John Donald Cameron

A Sketch of the Tobacco Interests in North Carolina

An Account of the Culture, Handling and Manufacture of the Staple

John Donald Cameron

A Sketch of the Tobacco Interests in North Carolina
An Account of the Culture, Handling and Manufacture of the Staple

ISBN/EAN: 9783337306595

Printed in Europe, USA, Canada, Australia, Japan

Cover: Foto ©Suzi / pixelio.de

More available books at **www.hansebooks.com**

—OF THE—

TOBACCO INTERESTS

—IN—

NORTH CAROLINA.

BEING AN ACCOUNT OF THE CULTURE, HANDLING AND MANUFAC-
TURE OF THE STAPLE; TOGETHER WITH SOME INFORMATION
RESPECTING THE PRINCIPAL FARMERS, MANUFACTURING
ESTABLISHMENTS AND WAREHOUSES; WITH STATIS-
TICS EXHIBITING THE GROWTH OF TOBACCO IN
THE WESTERN COUNTIES, AND ALSO IN THE
OTHER TOBACCO PRODUCING REGIONS
OF THE STATE, AS SHOWN BY COM-
PARISON OF THE CROP OF 1880
WITH THOSE OF PRECED-
ING YEARS.

BY J. D. CAMERON,

Editor of the Durham, N. C., Recorder.

OXFORD, N. C.,
W. A. DAVIS & CO., PUBLISHERS
1881.

BALTIMORE:
PRESS OF ISAAC FRIEDENWALD,
103 W. Fayette Street.

INTRODUCTION.

The caprices of human taste and appetite present most interesting subjects for consideration, for those caprices are connected most intimately
with human progress; with the spread of civilization, by the influence
they exert upon the intercourse of nations; and they define most dis-
tinctly the dividing line between the creature of intellect and the creature of
instinct; the one, in the gratification of appetite, or the satisfaction of
cravings, plunging boldly into the mysteries of nature, and snatching new
pleasures almost from the very jaws of death; coming out triumphant with
new treasures, and adding to the resources of human enjoyment, stores of
solace or of excitement, drawn from those things that pure animal instinct
rejects as noxious or hurtful. On the other hand, the habits and the tastes
of the brute creation remain unchanged throughout all time. The same
food and the same drink that satisfied their original progenitors, suffice for
the wants of their descendants, with the exception of certain limited
modifications, enforced by soil, climate or locality.

Man is called to account, by the philosopher of his own race, for the
presentation of such contrast, and condemned for his departure from the
simple rule of nature. But what we are pleased to call the simplicity of
nature, in our commendation of the superior wisdom of the brute, is, in
reality, the approval of a blind, inflexible law, imposed and enforced by
Creative Wisdom upon creatures without wisdom, beyond the limit of the
narrow but safe law of instinct. For mere physical perfection, the provision
for the brute may be the happier.

The liberty of man is unlimited. Set as lord and master over terrestrial
creation, his reason is his guide or his prompter to good and to evil. To
evil most largely; for as the animal part of his nature predominates, so
does it impel him to gratify animal appetites, and search out new secrets of
animal enjoyment. Investigating, exploring, subjugating in the domain of
appetite, he is no less inquisitive and tyrannical than he has been in his
other conquests. If it is a tribute to his intellectual power that his acqui-
sitions have been so large and so curious, it is somewhat of a rebuke to his
moral weakness that he becomes so often the victim of his own achievements.

It is very remarkable, in the notice of human habits, to find of how
recent origin or application is much of what is now inseparably associated
with the comfort and even the necessities of social existence. Almost all
the appliances of domestic luxury and of artificial stimulants are of modern

discovery, extraction or application. The ancients were, in their way, as self-indulgent as the moderns, far more extravagant in their devotion to appetite. They ate of the most costly viands, and they drank beverages that might turn their feasts into riots. But in the preparation of the first they knew nothing of the spices and condiments which give the zest to the modern table, and the latter they received almost ready-made from the hand of nature. The ready grape was prompt to convert its abundant juices into the generous wine, potent to cheer or to inebriate. But the more fiery beverages, owing their power to the artificial creation of alcohol, waited for modern chemical skill to call them into existence. The milder stimulus of tea and coffee was unknown to the luxury of the Roman and the Greek; nor was their food made grateful to the palate by the use of the sugar so indispensable to the modern cuisine. But in nothing was their ignorance so profound and so pitiable as in their want of knowledge of TOBACCO, the discovery of which marks a boundary between the past and the present of human habit, as sharp as might be presented by a contrast of the naked Pict and his modern successor, the enlightened and luxurious Briton. In the universality of its present use it is difficult to conceive of a time when it was not, as now, the common refuge and solace for all mankind, from the philosopher to the clown, from the refined Caucasian to the dusky savage, all greeting with avidity this new gift of heaven, and accepting with joy this new boon of geographical researches.

Perhaps nothing has proved so great a stimulus to the greed of conquest, the expansion of empire, the grasp of colonization, the spread of civilization and the activity of commerce, as the spur of appetite awaked by the knowledge of these newly found modern luxuries. The remotest regions of the earth were penetrated to procure them; the most active traffic was begotten to exchange for them, or the most determined wars were originated to secure them. And now, since regular channels have been provided for their procurement, or systematic cultivation adopted to supply them, they have become the great mainsprings of modern commercial enterprise and the great mainstays of modern manufacturing energies.

Giving to each one of the luxuries referred to its due share of consequence, and all its peculiar honors, there is no one of them which exacts so universal a tribute from the whole human race as

TOBACCO,

which throws its spell of enchantment over all mankind, and compels submission from all alike—from the peasant and the peer, from the millionaire and the mendicant; which elevates the philosopher, inspires the poet, animates the man of business, and cheers the slaves of toil; the chosen companion of the cheerful and the comforter of the sorrowful; alike sought after by all men, in all conditions and circumstances of life; a friend so general and so genial as to justify the poetic yet philosophical Bulwer in saying that, "He who doth not smoke, hath either known no great grief, or refuseth himself the softest consolation next to that which cometh from heaven."

Occupying so important a relation to the mental comfort of mankind, it is not surprising that it has stimulated industry and skill to minister to the universal demand upon its capabilities; that it has awakened the energies of agriculture, fanned the wings of commerce, and given birth to active manufacturing enterprise; that it has subdued the wilderness in its search for new fields of culture, created populations where silence had been wont to hold dominion, and called flourishing towns and cities into existence to demonstrate the power of an inanimate agency.)

It is not proposed in these introductory pages to go into a minute history of tobacco. If that is done, it will be in connection with the consideration of its varieties, its culture and its uses. A brief reference to its origin must here suffice. Nothing is more conclusive of its modern discovery and its American origin than the utter silence of all writers in regard to its existence previous to the discovery of America. Its almost instant adoption by the whole human race as soon as its virtues were made known, proves that the use of tobacco would not have been foregone had it been within reach. It was first heard of through the followers of Columbus, who noticed that the natives puffed smoke through their mouths and nostrils; and that they used a dried leaf which they placed in small clay pipes in which was inserted a hollow reed. The leaf was tobacco, and the pipe was the predecessor of the costly meerschaum. Not only was the use of the weed observed on the islands, but subsequently it was found in universal habit on both the northern and southern continents of America. To this day it may be found growing wild in the Western and Southern States of the American Union; and very recently a new and distinct variety has been discovered in Southern California among the ruins of the towns and habitations of a people long extinct, perpetuating itself from year to year by seeds dropped from each annual crop, and showing the uses to which it was once applied by being found in close proximity to large quantities of antiquated pipes, which could have had no other application. This is another proof of its American origin.

Sir Francis Drake, perhaps in his voyage of 1573, brought samples of tobacco into England. Sir Walter Raleigh had much to do with making it fashionable, and smoking became sufficiently popular and sufficiently general to draw forth that fierce counterblast of King James, who was as impotent in his royal wrath to drive back the tide of the new and seductive habit as his predecessor, Canute, had been to control by royal mandate the onward progress of the waves of the sea. This novel tide was to submerge not only England, but all the parts of the earth.

It has often been observed how many of human plans lead to results widely different and far remote from what was originally designed. Almost the sole incentive to the colonization of the new American shores was the discovery of gold, believed to exist in fabulous quantity in some as yet undiscovered part of the continent. When the sanguine colonists of Jamestown heard the result of their first shipment of the golden sands of James river, and learned that it was nothing more than worthless mica spangles, they may have consoled themselves under their bitter chagrin in the oblivious cloud of smoke from the soothing pipe, and learned at length that in the tobacco fields they had really, if unwittingly, found a true El Dorado. For, despairing of the discovery of the metallic gold, they sought it in the culture and sale of the weed which a new habit had made indispensable to human luxury or comfort, and which made returns that filled the coffers of the planters as effectively and substantially as the metallic representative. Gold was found above the soil, not under it; and henceforward the southern colonies went on to grow and to prosper, to become populous, wealthy and refined, and to reach that social and political height which gave them preëminent influence with the other colonies, and which has never been lost through the lapse of time, the shocks of war or the reverses of fortune. And this is all directly traceable to tobacco.

Tobacco was soon made to perform also the functions of gold in another form. Its culture once firmly established, and markets opened for its disposal, it became the common medium of exchange, the standard of value, and almost the sole currency of Virginia at least. It paid the taxes of the farmer, it liquidated his debts to the merchant, it satisfied the parson for his ministrations, and it measured the dowry of the bride. It was made in its earliest colonial days, as it has been made to do in the maturity of modern commonwealths, to bear a most important relation to the subject of revenue. King James, and his successor, King Charles, both strove to obtain a monopoly of the sale of tobacco raised in Virginia, which the Governor and Council compromised, by agreeing to contract with their sovereign for at least 500,000 pounds, at 3s. and 6d. per pound, to be inspected and guaranteed to be of uniform good quality, which is the origin of the present system of inspection. But this contract carried with it another burden opposed to the liberties of agriculture. That the sovereign might be freed from competition, and obtain full prices for the amount of tobacco delivered to him, the planter was required to gather only twelve leaves from each plant. In its early history, as in its modern experience, tobacco has been the sport of legislation, the subject of vexatious laws and tyrannical exactions, as if law-makers had conspired to punish mankind for the facility with which they had yielded to its seductive dominion.

North Carolina lagged many years behind Virginia in the extent of the culture of tobacco; for whereas all the tide-water region of the latter State became almost exclusively devoted to this staple, long before the Revolutionary War, but comparatively a small portion of the former was given up to it. The counties of Warren and Granville, and the counties along Dan, with portions of Orange and Chatham, under their former limits, were probably the only counties in which tobacco was extensively cultivated for market.

With the progress of settlement and with the acquisition of the territories beyond the Alleghanies and the Mississippi, lands and climate were both found by the Virginia and the North Carolina emigrant to induce experimental trials in those regions. How successfully, the vast production of Kentucky and Missouri has long furnished satisfactory proof. The other new western States and Territories, as they came into being, made the same ventures. The colder northern and northwestern States made the trial, and they too succeeded. The result is that there is scarcely a State in the Union which is not tobacco-growing to some extent.

In such wide diversity of soil and climate there must of necessity have been developed many varieties of quality ; and as a consequence we find the seed-leaf of Pennsylvania and Connecticut with a fragrance almost equal to the famous product of Cuba ; the rich and fragrant leaf of Virginia and North Carolina, unapproachable anywhere in the world as a chewing tobacco, and the foundation of those brands of smoking tobacco which find consumers everywhere in the reach of commerce. The heavier and darker qualities of Kentucky and Missouri have their peculiar excellencies and always find ready markets. The same may be said of Tennessee.

It is undeniable that North Carolina is the producer of tobacco unequalled even in Virginia ; and yet owing to the course trade has almost always taken, she is deprived of her due credit both for quantity and quality. Until within a few years, when she has built up some interior markets, Virginia has absorbed her fame as well as her products. The statistical tables of 1875 put North Carolina as the fourth State in extent of crop, yet foreign commercial tables take no note of this, and the forty or more millions of leaf tobacco that go out of North Carolina, go upon the world as Virginia tobacco. It is no reproach to Virginia that this is so. She has systematized her business by the experience of two centuries, and shipments from Richmond and Petersburg had a guarantee for their excellence in the fidelity, knowledge and skill of those who controlled the market. And Virginia had given North Carolina the only market within reach of her producing regions until that change in the system of sales, established since the war, has given her markets of her own. It is now her duty to show to the world what she does, and vindicate her fame and the magnitude of her resources.

How can she part with her property in the fame of her "bright yellow tobacco," a fame based upon its North Carolina origin and broadened by its almost exclusive North Carolina production ? The name of Marshall, who opened up the golden treasure of California, and gave birth, as it were, to the Empire State of the Pacific, ought not to be held in higher honor than that of Capt. Abishai Slade, of Caswell county, who, in 1856, made that discovery by which the dark brown leaf of tobacco was turned by magic touch into a foliage

Shining as patines of bright gold,"

a color marvellous to the uninitiated ; a color that inspires the seller to hold on to his wares with a kind of covetous greed ; a color that fascinates and excites the buyer as if he could not pay too much for this beautiful semblance of the product of the mine.

Now all this treasure is almost exclusively in possession of our State. Until recently it was confined to the narrow belt running from southeast to northwest—embracing portions of the counties of Warren, Granville, Orange, Person, Caswell, Alamance and Rockingham, and reaching a little way over into Virginia. Now that area has been extended by the addition of the extreme eastern counties of Wayne and Lenoir, of the middle counties of Stokes and Forsythe, of the western counties of Catawba, Iredell and McDowell, and the trans-montane counties of Buncombe, Madison, Haywood, Henderson, Yancey and Transylvania.

It is a monopoly of the most magnificent kind ; a monopoly of a production without a rival and of a market without a competitor ; yet it goes abroad in its crude form as Virginia tobacco, and the world hears nothing of North Carolina in connection with it.

Without doing injustice to our sister State, or prejudicing her just claims to priority in so much that concerns tobacco in all its relations to agriculture, to commerce, to manufacture and to legislation, the just claims of North Carolina will be presented in these pages, with the hope that a State pride, defective in so much else, may be aroused to vindicate her reputation in this, one of her most important interests.

A SKETCH

OF

THE TOBACCO INTERESTS OF NORTH CAROLINA.

CHAPTER I.

GEOLOGICAL FEATURES—THE WINSTON SECTION.

WHILE tobacco, as a native plant of America, will readily grow in almost all parts of North Carolina, it has long been well known that the finer qualities are restricted to certain limits defined by characteristic geological peculiarity. And it is curious to notice that this limit is fixed by one geological formation; and that in all parts of that system the results prove to be the same. For years after the discovery of the mode of curing the "bright yellow tobacco," custom, and at length steady belief, had restricted those limits within the narrow bounds of a few favored counties; and the favorable results of experiments made beyond that zone were ascribed rather to accident than to similarity in the elements of soil essential to the perfect development of such product; or such product was disparaged as wanting in *all*, if possessing *some*, of the merits of the fruits of the favored region. One of the beneficent results of the State Geological Survey, a work yet incomplete, derided, opposed and threatened with summary suppression, was to demonstrate the wide extent of the *Laurentian System.* Practical experience had proved the special adaptation of certain soils to the production of the finer kinds of tobacco. Science stepped in to confirm the judgment of experience, and to give confidence to the bold adventurer who might dare to step beyond prescribed limitations.

The characteristics of this system, one of the oldest of the series of stratified rocks, are, that they contain most of the metamorphic rocks of North Carolina, "consisting of granite, syenite and other horn-blendic rocks, dionite and crystalline limestone; and these contain much magnetic and specular iron ore, frequently in many large beds; and beds of graphite are also common." *

The map of the Geological Survey of North Carolina shows the extent,

---

* Kerr's Geology of North Carolina, p. 113.

and also the wide separation of this system by the interposition of other formations. It makes its appearance about the centre of the State, embracing a portion of the counties of Wake, Granville, Orange, Alamance, Caswell, Person, and Rockingham, and extending some distance over into Virginia into the counties of Halifax and Pittsylvania. This has been preeminently the treasure-house of the bright yellow tobacco. But again, it makes its appearance, after a separation by broad belts of miocene and taconic formation, at a point beginning near Wentworth, in Rockingham County, and extending in a southwestern course nearly to the South Carolina line, and reaching nearly to the foot of the Blue Ridge; and here again is found another field for the production of "bright yellow" tobacco. Again it reappears beyond the Blue Ridge, occupying most of the mountain plateau between that range and the Smoky Mountains; and in the counties of Buncombe, Madison, Yancey, Haywood, and others adjacent, is found a new field for this valuable production.

It is thus evident that a special subject of industry must expand far beyond the limits to which it was believed to be rigidly restricted; with this difference, that while that portion of the geologic system beyond the Blue Ridge is adapted apparently only to light and highly colored tobaccos, those portions to the east of it have a wider latitude of variety, and produce with equal excellence the dark and heavy grades in demand for the worker of plug stock, and the bright and highly priced finer qualities in request for smokers and wrappers.

In this treatise it is proposed to consider these sections in the order in which they present themselves, beginning at the eastern limit of the western section, and giving information in detail so far as obtained.

THE WINSTON SECTION.

This properly embraces the counties of Stokes and Forsythe, of Davie and Davidson, and involves to large extent those of Guilford and Rockingham. The surface is undulating, sometimes boldly so; again stretching out in broad, comparatively level areas. The native growth includes many varieties of oak, hickory, chestnut, walnut, dogwood and chinquepin; the woods in parts being quite open, in others filled with dense undergrowth. The soil varies more in color than in chemical structure. In portions of Forsythe, for instance, it is gray, light and friable; while in another it is dark or reddish, and heavier and more compact; but all exhibiting the same results, analyses probably showing large percentages of potash or of alkali and alkaline earth, the darker portions tinged with the oxides of iron, but all proving their adaptability to the production of tobacco in its most perfect form.

The cultivation of tobacco in this section is no new thing. For many years it had been pursued on the richer and heavier lands, with the only aim of application to the coarse grades of plug tobacco, much of which was manufactured at home by the farmer in a very primitive method, the presses being in the open air, worked by a screw operated by the long wing-levers once familiar to the eye in the cotton regions. The curing was in the same primitive style, air or sun curing being universal. It may be a question if the lover of good chewing tobacco has not lost by the modern processes, which sacrifice flavor to color, and which give to the eye that which they deny to the palate.

But in this section there was no expansion in cultivation, because the production being the fruits of a rich, rank soil, could not come in competition with those of a soil yet richer and ranker and more extended in area, such as is abundantly found in Virginia and Maryland, in Kentucky and Missouri. It was after the discovery of the process of curing tobacco to a bright yellow was introduced, that experiment proved these lands as well suited to the production of that as well as to a high grade of dark tobacco suitable to dark wrappers and fillers as any other in the State; and with the facility of markets built up in the centre of the producing region, and manufactories springing into existence to keep alive a permanent demand, the industry now engages the interest of many counties until lately wholly ignorant of the culture or even of the various qualities of tobacco.

WINSTON.

Forsythe County, cut off from the county of Stokes, was formed in 1848, and Winston, immediately contiguous to the somewhat venerable town of Salem, was made county-seat. For more than twenty years after its designation as the county capital, it had no other importance. Salem overshadowed it by its older population, its large mercantile transactions and its educational reputation. Winston lived in humble obscurity as a courthouse village, until suddenly the spring was touched which gave her life and energy, and made her a name more widely and interestedly known than that of her venerable sister. She has now a population of little less than four thousand, a town handsomely and substantially built, and a business, based upon the sales and manufacture of tobacco, which makes it one of the most important centres of that stupendous interest.

In the town of Winston there are three sales warehouses, fourteen plug factories, one smoking factory, not at present in operation, and one plug factory, so immediately in the vicinity as properly may be included in the interests of the town. A brief sketch of each will be given in detail, together with information, as far as could be obtained, of such points and establishments as are practically tributary to the business of Winston. And first of the warehouses,

BROWN'S WAREHOUSE.

In 1872, Mr. T. J. Brown was encouraged by the increasing cultivation of tobacco in this section, to venture upon the enterprise of opening a, warehouse in Winston, which he did in an old barn of small size, 30x40 feet. The sales were advertised to take place daily, but supplies were irregular and small, and sale days were few and far between. There was then only one plug factory in the place, whose yearly output was not more than twenty thousand pounds. The culture in the surrounding country was small, conducted in primitive methods, without the use of artificial fertilizers, and curing was effected by the air or the sun or by wood fires. The introduction of coal curing, and more recently of flues, has completely revolutionized the whole system, the result of which is the abundant production of fine yellow tobacco, as well as a very superior article of dark grades. The increase of production compelled an increase of accommodations, and Brown's warehouse is now a building 70x200, with full skylight and abundant conveniences within and without. The sales take place daily during the season. The house is known under the name of T. J. Brown & Co., and is formed by Messrs. T. J. Brown, W. B. Carter and J. R. Pearce. Mr. R. D. Moseley is auctioneer and Mr. P. A. Wilson book-keeper.

Mr. Brown reports that the condition of the growing crop is very superior, and greatly increased in quantity. Many new men have gone into the business this year, and older planters have enlarged their operations. In characterizing peculiarities, he describes the tobacco of Stokes County as remarkably rich and waxy. He estimates the sales of Winston for the current year at seven millions of pounds, of which home manufacturers take about one-half; the remainder is bought on orders for Canada, the Western cities, Baltimore, etc., some large houses in the latter city, such as Gail & Ax, obtaining a large proportion of their stock here.

Mr. Brown adds that when he embarked in business in 1872 there were no banks in Winston, and no facilities whatever to aid a struggling enterprise. All this is now changed, there being ample bank accommodations, and also the convenient addition of a revenue office. The growth of the town in size and in business is more marked within the past five years than at any previous period.

The next warehouse in date of erection is that of

PHOL & STOCKTON.

The house, built in 1874 by W. A. Lash, was known as "Lash's Warehouse." It was subsequently occupied by Norwood & Pearce, who were succeeded by Haines & Brown, then by Cabell & Hairston, then by Sheppard & Wiles; and about July 1st of the present year (1880) it passed into the possession of the present proprietors, Phol & Stockton. The building is of wood, 70x200, well lighted, and with ample accommodations; those for wagons and horses being now largely increased. Mr. John Sheppard, formerly of Richmond, afterwards of Danville, is general business manager. He has been a warehouseman since 1865, and inherits a family instinct which has given to Richmond so many men distinguished in tobacco life.

Mr. Sheppard reports the estimated annual sales at this warehouse at two million of pounds. The bulk of receipts are fine wrappers, both bright and mahogany, and fillers. The counties in North Carolina tributary to Winston are Forsythe, Stokes, Surry, Yadkin, Rowan, Davie, Davidson, Iredell, Wilkes, Guilford, and Rockingham; and Virginia is largely represented by Patrick Henry and Grayson counties. Stokes and Davie stand at the head of the market for superiority in all grades; the fine tobaccos of these counties, and of Guilford, compare favorably with the best made in Granville. Mr. Sheppard thinks the tobacco of this section better suited to all general purposes than any other part of the country; and there is eager and steady demand from the North, the West, and from Canada, which has the effect of maintaining always a firm market.

The soil of the lower or southern part of Forsythe is light sandy loam; the upper part and that of Stokes, red and heavier; the growth oak, hickory, chestnut, etc., with undergrowth of chinquepin; in some parts the woods open and covered with grass. The lands in Davie and Davidson are chocolate-colored loam, and almost entirely free from rock.

The firm of Phol & Stockton is composed of T. A. Wiles, floor manager; N. T. Stockton, bookkeeper; E. Phol, financial agent, and James Stockton, general supervisor.

The Piedmont Warehouse

was established by Hobson & Scales as the Planter's Warehouse. Mr. M. W. Norfleet took charge of the house in 1876, and gave it its present title, and increased its capacity to 14,200 square feet, with ample accommodations; wagons unload inside of the building, and there is a wagon-shed 190x20. The sales are held daily. The first year's sales did not exceed half a million pounds. They are now more than four times as great, and the increase this year is from 50 to 75 per cent. over that of the last.

Large orders are made to this house from distant points—from Detroit, from Louisville, Cincinnati, St. Louis, Baltimore, and from Canada. The large house of Gail & Ax, Baltimore, has been purchasing here for the past five years.

Fillers as fine as any made in the United States can be abundantly had here; the best from Stokes, which, in addition to some peculiar virtue of soil, has had the benefit of the longest experience. Mahogany wrappers of superior excellence, and lugs and smokers of remarkable sweetness and flavor, fill the market; and there is a fair proportion of bright wrappers and smokers.

Mr. M. W. Norfleet is the head of this house and general supervisor, Mr. W. A. S. Pearce is bookkeeper, Mr. James S. Scales floor manager, and Mr. J. Q. A. Barham auctioneer.

FACTORIES.

Culture and manufactures react the one upon the other. The first, finding a ready demand for its product, is stimulated to increased industry and encouraged to the application of higher skill. The other, obtaining its supplies with certainty and convenience, ventures to enlarge its operations, and becomes ambitious to expand its profits and its reputation. Such has been emphatically the case in Winston, where supply and demand have gone hand in hand; where the producer found a market when his products were ready for it, and where the consumer obtained his supplies without going far beyond his own doors to seek them. And that these supplies have been of superior excellence is proven by the fact that the fabrics of the Winston factories have so impressed their good qualities upon purchasers that the factories there have been spared during this year the mortification of suspended operations or short time, such as rival towns have been forced to submit to. On the contrary, the Winston factories have been worked to their utmost capacity to meet a constantly increasing demand. This is the testimony of the whole of them, as will be seen in the notice given of each one, and is the result of skill in manufacture, and of the perfect adaptation of the raw material used to the end sought to be attained.

One of the most extensive factories is that of

BROWN & BROTHER,

who worked under the same firm name in Mocksville, N. C., as far back as 1858, but who subsequently removed to Winston. They occupy a brick building, four stories high, exclusive of a commodious attic, 50x200 feet. It is perfectly arranged for the business, with every possible appliance for convenience and for safety; the large "dry rooms" being separated from the other part of the working space by fire-proof partitions. Hydraulic power in connection with steam is used for the press work. Two hundred and twenty-five hands are employed, during eight months of the year, in making all styles and grades of plug and twist; the latter being a specialty for the Southern and Western trade.

The production for the current year will reach five hundred thousand pounds, and, with continued proportionate increase of business, is expected to reach one million pounds next year.

The prominent brands of this factory are " Honest 7," " Cottage Home," " Waverly," " Ruby," " Little Joker," " Archer," " Brick Factory," " Golden Link," " Gold Dust," " Oliver Twist," " H W's." " Slap Jack," " Dexter," " Brown's Mule," etc. " Oliver Twist " is a popular brand of twist.

The Messrs. Brown report that Winston is not so good a market in which to obtain brights as fillers; in which last there has been in recent years marked improvement, and they are little, if at all, inferior to the noted Henry (Va.) County fillers. For fine wrappers, Davie, Davidson, and Rockingham counties are most approved.

P. H. HAINES & Co.

began work in 1874. They occupy a brick building 118x55, with an extension wing 105 feet long, the main building being four stories high. Hydraulic power, applied by steam, is used. One hundred and seventy-five hands, including forty-five rollers, are employed, who will turn out half a million of pounds this season, with a constantly increasing demand; and there is an expectation of a much larger production next year. The usual sizes of plug and twist are made for a large trade extending from Baltimore to Texas, including all the intermediate States South and West. Last year a considerable quantity of the manufacture of this house was sent to Kansas, and it gains favor wherever used.

This house is composed of energetic and sagacious young men, intelligent and sagacious in their business, and shrewd and enterprising to adopt every possible improvement, thus maintaining and advancing a reputation gained by attentive skill — keeping abreast with all rivalry, resulting in operations the extent of which is not surpassed by any similar establishment in North Carolina.

BYRUM, COTTON & JONES

opened in 1879, the firm being composed of Taylor Byrum, Robert Cotton and E. D. Jones. They occupy a brick building three and half stories high, and 40x100, and use hydraulic power in pressing. They employ about sixty hands, including fifteen rollers, and make plug and twist; of the former, from 6x3 to 12x3; and of the latter, six and twelve inch. Among their prominent brands are Wachowa, Silver Wave, Smart Aleck, Mamie Lee, Shoe Heel, and Oneida. The amount annually made is about one hundred and twenty-five thousand pounds, with a steadily progressive increase. The trade of this house is now spread over ten States: Ohio, Maryland, Virginia, the two Carolinas, Georgia, Alabama, Mississippi and Florida. All stock for this factory is obtained on the Winston market.

C. HAMLIN & Co.,

successors to C. Hamlin, began business in 1872. Their building is brick, two and a half stories, and is 40x100. They employ about sixty hands, including twelve rollers, using improved machinery, and turn out annually about one hundred and twenty-five thousand pounds of the usual sizes and grades of plug and twist. Their trade is principally with Baltimore and the South. Like all the other houses in Winston, this one shows a constantly increasing business.

T. L. VAUGHAN & Co.

Mr. T. L. Vaughan, though not the first manufacturer in Winston, erected its first tobacco factory. The present firm was organized in 1878. It occupies a brick building 118x53, with an "L" of 58 feet long, also of brick, the whole two and a half stories high, and is practically three stories high.   One hundred and twenty-five hands are employed, including twenty-eight rollers, who produce annually two hundred and fifty thousand pounds of the usual sizes and grades of plug and twist.   The trade is principally with the South, though large shipments are made to Cincinnati and Memphis.   The business of this firm is also increasing, and the product next year is expected to exceed largely that of the present one.

BITLING & WHITAKER,

in the extent of their operations, and in the repute of their product, are second to no house in Winston.   They began work in that town in 1876, and occupy a building of wood, four stories high and 40x116.   The annual capacity of the house is five hundred thousand pounds, which will probably be exceeded this year, and certainly so the next.   It employs about two hundred and twenty-five hands, who turn out all grades of plug and twist, for which an active demand is found, principally in the South and South-west, and also in Baltimore and Cincinnati.   This firm are the manufacturers of the brands celebrated as " Lucille," " Empress," and "Sprig of Acacia."

W. W. WOOD

built his factory in 1877, and began work in 1878.   His building is of brick, four stories high, and is 40x140.   He employs one hundred and twenty-five hands, who this year will produce two hundred and fifty thousand pounds nett tobacco.   The first year his products were sixty-five thousand pounds, the second year two hundred thousand, and the current year as above stated.   But Mr. Wood, by a happy invention, will hereafter largely surpass, in all probability, any result he has as yet attained.   With high inventive genius, he has patented a mill which is designed to pack tobacco in new and very attractive forms, the mill pressing into the " shapes " the lumps, which form a central decagon, from which extend the corresponding radical pieces, the diameter over all being about twelve inches, and the whole neatly packed in an oaken bucket containing forty-five pounds, and appropriately branded " The Old Oaken Bucket."   The style is so novel and beautiful that the eyes of the trade have been strongly drawn toward it ; and the demand for the new style is already so great that Mr. Wood will probably abandon altogether the hardly less ' celebrated brands of " Mark Twain " and " Maud Muller," and devote his efforts exclusively to " The Old Oaken Bucket."   Mr. Wood has been engaged in the tobacco business in many of its various branches throughout his business life.

HAMILTON SCALES,

better known as Ham. Scales, began the manufacture of tobacco in Winston in 1870, and was the pioneer of the business.   There being no sales warehouse in the place at that time, his supplies were obtained by direct transactions with the planters on their farms.   He erected his present factory of wood in 1875. It is 2½ stories high, 60x34, with a cooling room 34x18, and dry-house 16x16. He works on an average fifty hands, producing annually one hundred and twenty-five thousand pounds of plug altogether, the most prominent brands of which are " Aleck Stephens," " No. 1," in 30 pound packages, " Bob Toombs" and " Piedmont." His trade is principally with the South, with uniform steady increase.

BAILEY BROTHERS,

consisting of W. D. Bailey and P. N. Bailey, removed from Statesville, where they had worked as manufacturers since 1874, to Winston during the year 1880. They occupy a building of wood, three stories high, 35x70, and employ fifty hands, turning out one hundred thousand pounds of plug and twist. Their trade, constantly increasing, is mostly with the Southern States.

P. W. DALTON & CO.,

the firm being composed of P. W. Dalton, W. J. Cooper and Lee Hendricks. They began work during the current year, 1880, in a building of wood, two and one-half stories high, and 40x50, with a dry-house 20 feet in length. They employ on an average through the working season fifty hands, who will make this year one hundred and fifty thousand pounds of nett tobacco of all the styles and grades of plug and twist. Owing to the steady increase of demand, this house expects next year to increase its production to two hundred and fifty thousand pounds. Its trade is mostly with South Carolina, Georgia and Alabama, with scattering transactions with all the territory from Virginia to Texas. The most prominent brands are " P. W. Dalton," " Little Harry," " Little Gracie," " Little Nina," " Old Virginia," " Orange Leaf," " Rose Bud," " Yellow Jessamine," " Geranium," and " P. W. Dalton's A. A. A. A."

R. J. REYNOLDS

began business at his present location in 1874, gradually enlarging his building as his business increased, until he now occupies a brick building, 38x128, three stories high, and employing one hundred and twenty-five hands, with a nett result of two hundred and seventy-five thousand pounds for the current working year. The steady increase of business will compel additions to the buildings next year. The trade is partly with the South, but more extensive with the North and West, exacting a great variety of styles and grades for so many different markets. The prominent brands are " Strawberry," twist ; " Oronoko," pounds ; " World's Choice," pounds ; and Reynolds' " Bright 7 ounce twist."

H. H. REYNOLDS

began business this year, 1880, in a building partly brick, partly wood, 38x110, and two and one-half stories high. He employs between sixty-five and seventy hands, making one hundred thousand pounds nett tobacco, exclusively twist. The trade is with both North and South and is exclusively wholesale, and the attention of this house is largely given to working up jobbers' brands.

Mr. Reynolds reports as a general feature of the business in Winston, that the "Little Oronoko" is mostly used for fillers, and the "Broad Oronoko" and "Silky Pryor" for wrappers. A new and apparently accidental variety locally known as "Sea" is coming into use in the counties along the Virginia border. It prizes a dark rich color.

From two other factories in Winston, and from one in the vicinity, no information was obtained. Their aggregate annual production of plug and twist is estimated at three hundred and fifty thousand pounds.

Besides the factories in the town of Winston, there are many points within a comparatively short distance, and most of which purchase their stocks in the Winston market. Chief among these is

MOUNT AIRY,

in Surry County, which is in the centre of a fine tobacco country, the products of which are "brights" of fine color and quality, and very superior "mahogany." Curing is effected by coal and by flues, the latter coming into more favor, and there is a great demand for Lyon's sheet-iron flue.

A warehouse was opened at Mount Airy a few years ago, but was soon abandoned as such and converted into a factory. There are three factories in the town, to wit: those of Messrs. Brower, Banner, and Ashley; and within a radius of four miles of the town four more, those of Messrs. Sparker, Patterson, R. L. Gwynn, and Fulton. The nett aggregate product of the whole of the above is about five hundred thousand pounds.

KERNERSVILLE,

in Forsythe County, has five factories, producing in the aggregate about three hundred thousand pounds of plug and twist. The manufacturers are Messrs. King, Leake, Beard, Roberts & Co., and Kerner, all with good and increasing business.

BETHANIA,

in Forsythe County, was long ago widely known as the seat of the extensive cigar factory of Lash & Bros. That has long been closed, but has been succeeded by the plug and twist factory of O. J. Lehman & Co., who make about one hundred thousand pounds yearly; and in the vicinity is the factory of C. H. Orender, who makes about seventy-five thousand pounds of the same.

D. W. Dalton, in Stokes County, twenty miles from Winston, makes of plug and twist about one hundred thousand pounds.

N. D. Sullivan, at Walkertown, in Forsythe County, is one of the most noted manufacturers in the county, his work being uniformly fine. He is remarkable for his strict adherence to his prices, not permitting his agents to sell for more than the sum he had fixed, even though there had been an advance in the market.

Piggott & Co., at High Point, Guilford County, have a plug factory which produces between seventy-five thousand and one hundred thousand annually.

At Walnut Cove, in Stokes County. Dr. Wm. Lash has a plug factory with a yearly capacity of about seventy-five thousand pounds.

At Mocksville, H. B. Howard & Co. have a plug factory with about the same capacity ;

And Payne, Lunn & Co., at Salisbury, have a plug factory turning out about two hundred thousand pounds a year.

AGGREGATE PRODUCTION.

This can only be ascertained approximately. The three warehouses in Winston only estimate their sales ; but suppose them to reach seven millions of pounds for the crop season closing with the month of September, 1880, the manufacture of nett tobacco in the Winston factories reaches 3,275,000 lbs., to which may be added ten per cent. for stems, which gives 3,602,500.

The factories at Mount Airy, Kernersville and elsewhere in the surrounding country, obtain most of their stock in Winston, and this will add at least one million more to the receipts of the Winston warehouses. To this must be added the very large amount bought on orders and shipped in the leaf, and also the large quantity shipped on speculation. The aggregate will therefore exceed, rather than fall below, the estimated receipts of the warehousemen.

All accounts coincide as to the excellent condition of the growing crop, and the large increase in area planted. No account places it less than twenty-five per cent., and therefore the receipts on the Winston market for the next year will fall little short of ten million pounds.

REVENUE RECEIPTS.

Dr. W. H. Wheeler, the Collector for the 5th District, kindly furnishes the following amounts paid on Tobacco for the year ending June 30th, 1880, in the different counties composing the district:

Alamance	$ 538	56
Caswell	15,846	60
Forsythe	314,998	82
Guilford	24,460	68
Person	49,204	84
Rockingham	244,930	67
Randolph	2,860	08
Stokes	70,008	70
Surry	78,486	62

Total......$801,335 57

CHAPTER II.

STATESVILLE SECTION.

A LTHOUGH no market has been permanently opened at this point, its relation to the rapidly developing culture of tobacco in Iredell and adjoining counties, naturally tributary to a point commanding such superior facilities for transportation as Statesville, makes the existence of one only a question of time.

The geological structure of this section is also the Upper Laurentian; and its similarity in general features attracted the attention of tobacco planters from the counties of Person and Caswell, who foresaw the fruit that awaited judicious experiment. That experiment has been made and with success, and the culture of tobacco now engages the attention of the farmers of Iredell, as well as those of Alexander, Caldwell, Mitchell, Wilkes, Yancey, and others who possess like characteristics of soil and climate.

Mr. R. J. West, of Statesville, engaged in the tobacco business for many years, and at present a partner in a warehouse at Hickory, furnishes the following information:

The culture of tobacco in this section as a market crop was undertaken since the war. The inducement to it was the similarity in soil to that of the lands in Caswell County which produced the bright yellow tobacco. Settlers from that and other similarly situated counties came to Iredell, some as instructors in the mysteries of curing, but the majority as permanent citizens of a virgin territory. Thirty or forty families from these counties are engaged in the cultivation. Their success has been marked, the result being a rich, large, bright yellow tobacco, inferior to the best Caswell tobacco only in texture. Fine dark wrappers and good rich fillers are made.

The production this year in Iredell County is estimated at a million and a half of pounds, the increase over last year being several hundred per cent., and success will lead to a future wide expansion of the crop. The market for this has been divided between Hickory and Winston, but Hickory will be the chief market for the incoming crop. Shipments have been made to Danville, and more or less of the crop will always seek distant markets.

Little or no tobacco is raised in the southern part of the county, but in all other parts the culture is rapidly increasing. One immediate effect has been the increased value of lands, which have risen from three dollars an acre to ten dollars and upwards.

The counties tributary to Statesville are reported to be making rapid strides in tobacco culture. In Caldwell and Alexander Counties the lands are thought even better than in Iredell, and Wilkes County is represented as superior to all of these, and, in all, the increase in the crop this year is estimated at at least one thousand per cent.

In Mitchell County, which is north of the Blue Ridge, and which is broken and mountainous, the area north of the North Toe (properly Estato) River is considered specially adapted to fine yellow tobacco, being identical, in fact, with the lands of Madison County, hereafter to be referred to.

Much attention is paid to the improvement of the plant. The Messrs. Deake, of Bakersville, introduced the Yellow Oronoko and Silky Pryor. Tobacco of low grade had been cultivated for many years, but it was not until the introduction of better seed that attention was given to curing. This is as yet imperfect, but a crop from this county, sold in the Lynchburg market, was pronounced by French and Italian buyers the best they had ever seen. The prominent farmers in this county, who may be regarded as the pioneers of its tobacco interests, are Selden and Garrett Bailey, and others of that name in Hollow Poplar township. Albert Slagle in Red Hill township has the largest crop in the county; John Peterson has a large crop, and —— M'Kinney one which is described as "extra fine."

In Yancey County, west of and adjoining Mitchell, and identical with it in natural features, there is a considerable quantity of tobacco raised on Jack and Pig Pen Creeks, and also on Carey River, which finds favor in the Marshall and Ackerville markets. In this county the production of tobacco increases with marvellous rapidity, and will soon absorb all agricultural interest, as it is the only crop which will profitably bear transportation in the absence of all railroad facilities.

WAREHOUSE AND FACTORY IN STATESVILLE.

There has not been in this place the energy of enterprise to meet the industry of the planter which distinguished Winston. One warehouse, of full capacity and excellent arrangement, was suffered to be closed through bad management; it is probable that it will be opened the coming season. There is only one factory in operation, that of Mr. McElwee, which makes both plug and smoking tobacco, both on a small scale. Mr. Thomas J. Bennett, from Franklin County, Va., is foreman, and worked a plug factory in Charlotte in 1858, and was subsequently with the factory of Dr. Keene at Salisbury.

H. L. Ayres is a manufacturer of cigars in Statesville, but uses Connecticut tobacco exclusively.

It is impossible that such advantages of position and proximity to so large and excellent a source of supply can be neglected by the business men of Statesville, who in all else are models of energy and sagacity; therefore their shortcomings are noted, not in condemnation, but with surprise.

CHAPTER III.

HICKORY AND ITS TRIBUTARY INTERESTS.

HICKORY, in Catawba County, is a railroad creation, springing up on the site of the "Old Hickory Tavern," the ruins of which, in the centre of the busy life and fresh-looking buildings of the new town, are reverently preserved, both as a memento of humble origin and as an eloquent note of progress. The situation of Hickory on the Western North Carolina Railroad is a commanding one, being the convenient shipping point for part of the adjoining county of Burke, of Caldwell, Alexander, the upper part of Iredell, parts of Wilkes, Watauga, and McDowell; and it became the centre of the large miscellaneous trade which developed it rapidly into the dimensions of a very thrifty town. Tobacco is soon destined to rank as its most important subject of business.

The country around Hickory is rolling, falling away somewhat boldly on the south and southwest towards the outlying spurs of the South Mountains; less boldly towards the north and northwest, where it expands itself in gently undulating folds; the whole covered with a not very dense growth of oak, hickory, chestnut and pine, with an undergrowth of dogwood, gumwood and chinquepin. The soil is sandy or gravelly loam, gray, with yellow or reddish clayey subsoil; with few rocks, and they in process of disintegration. The general appearance of soil and growth readily suggests to the practised eye a perfect adaptability to the culture of superior tobacco, and experience has confirmed such judgment.

But the culture as a market crop is of very recent introduction and of slow development, the most rapid advance having been made within the last three years.

Mr. J. K. Bobbitt, a former Granville planter, furnishes the following information:

He removed from Granville in 1875, and settled in the county of Burke, near the Catawba line, and within a few miles of Hickory; his object being to make fine yellow tobacco on lands he believed equal to the choicest lands in Granville County. His success has been complete; his crop last year averaged $22.50, and he made thirteen hundred and seventy-nine pounds on one and a half acres. He thinks that the plant has a quicker growth and more perfect maturity than in Caswell or Granville; is subject to few diseases, and is altogether free from "spot," which he ascribes to cooler and moister nights; but worms are as troublesome here as elsewhere. He also thinks tobacco is more readily cured bright here than in Granville, and that it possesses equal weight. More matured experience in culture, curing and handling, he thinks, will make it equal to the best.

In this vicinity the progress of culture is readily traced. In 1878, those who made a crop for market were Captain R. B. Davis, Addison Morgan and John D. Morgan. In 1879, in addition to these were L. A. Bolling, J. A. Hartsell, F. A. Wiley. C. M. White, Mrs. Holden, M. Martin, P. B. Summers, —— Huffman, and perhaps others. In 1880 there is a large addition to the number of planters, as well as a large increase in the crop planted by each; among whom are D. W. Rowe, 20 acres; D. Abernathy, 12 acres; R. B. Davis, 10 acres; R. W. McComb, 10 acres; and J. A. Hartsell has doubled his crop. F. A. Wiley, this year, as last, has 5 acres planted within the corporate limits of Hickory. In addition to the above are A. Morgan, 15 acres; J. D. Morgan, 5 acres, and P. K. Morgan, 6 acres: all within four miles of Hickory, in which area there are altogether 240 acres planted in tobacco this year.

The counties tributary to Hickory are all increasing their production in like proportion. In Caldwell County, north of the Catawba river, it is estimated that two-thirds of the land is suitable to find tobacco, and the cultivation is rapidly increasing. Among the principal planters are W. P. Mangum and W. O. Mangum, 10 acres each: Charles Satterthwaite, 15 acres; Sam Scheares and Chris. Satterthwaite, together, 20 acres; the widow Scheares, 10 acres; Daniel Hickman, 7 acres; A. Martin, 5 acres; Babel Sherrill, 5 acres, and many others; and most of the above are from the counties of Granville, Caswell and Person.

In Burke County, near its eastern border, are found J. K. Bobbitt, 3 acres; Hannibal Adams, 7 acres; —— Morgan, 10 acres; Hugh Ervin, 3 acres; Wm. Adams, 3 acres; Ephraim Aby, 4 acres; Aaron Cook, 2 acres, and others; these being also mostly from the counties east. Beyond the Catawba river, in the northern portion of Burke, the tobacco impulse is general; and the greater portion of the county will eventually be cultivated in that staple, a course justified by analysis of soils having a large percentage of lime and potash, elements favorable to the production of good tobacco.

Wilkes County increases its crop this year by several hundred per cent., with a quality of tobacco said to be equal to that of Granville. The same is said of Alexander County. McDowell County makes a very fine bright tobacco, but there has not been the same increase as in the counties already named. A considerable interest has been roused in Lincoln County, on the south, and the product is a very good bright.

Mr. J. K. Bobbitt claims to have been the first to erect a tobacco-barn in the county of Burke, and deserves honor for an example since so extensively followed. The increase in the value of lands in this county has been very decided, the advance being from three and five dollars to ten, fifteen dollars and upwards per acre.

In connection with the progress of the tobacco industries of this section, it seems proper to give in his own language copious extracts from information furnished by Mr. J. G. Hall, of Hickory, a manufacturer, and also warehouse proprietor, a man of intelligence and active enterprise, to whose energies the new town of Hickory owes much of its rapid advance. He says: "The progress of tobacco culture in Catawba and adjoining counties, with their centre of trade at Hickory, has not been rapid, but continuous. Prior to 1877, little or no attention had been paid to it. It is true that, up to that time, the firm of Marshall, Lancie & Co., afterwards A. W. Marshall, . had engaged in the manufacture of tobacco at Hickory, and here and there over the county might be found a man who, coming from the central tobacco regions of the State, attracted here, no doubt, by *the finest climate in North Carolina*, would cling to his first love and endeavor to raise tobacco. These first planters may rightfully be styled the ' Pioneers of Tobacco' upon the eastern slopes of the Blue Ridge, the true Piedmont region. Their success, limited as it was, was sufficient to attract attention, and to give good foundation for the belief of a few of our citizens that ' the culture of tobacco' actually belonged to this section of the State, and continuously through the past three years this faith in our soil and climate has been proved by works, and all our most intelligent planters ask is a little more time and experience to place them side by side with the most successful agriculturists in North Carolina. . . .

"We shall give the practical result of this confidence. In January, 1877, Messrs. Hall Bros., merchants in Hickory, N. C., conceived the idea of stimulating the culture of tobacco by the erection of a sales warehouse, which was made ready for business in February of the same year. The sales of this warehouse, the first in North Carolina west of Salisbury, were of necessity small, reaching only sixty thousand pounds during the season of 1877, and then followed in 1878 the *block up* of all the tobacco markets with the very large crop produced in the old tobacco regions in 1877. The immense production of that year, largely of a very common article, depressed prices to a greater degree than known for many years before or since, and had a depressing effect upon those among us who had hoped for a home market, the result of which was a partial abandonment of the culture the next year in some counties, particularly in McDowell, though since then it has been resumed.

"In 1878 the sales at Hall's warehouse amounted to about one hundred thousand pounds; but this did not properly represent the amount of production, for any one familiar with the history of new tobacco markets is aware that none can control at once more than a portion of the crop of the surrounding country. Our market entered the lists against such formidable rivals as Danville, Winston, Durham, and Lynchburg. Against such competition we are happy to say, to-day, that with five factories in Hickory, and the possibility of others next spring, we shall have a good demand for all the manufacturing stock that the season will produce.

"In 1879 Hickory handled about one hundred and fifty thousand pounds.

In February of the present year (1880) another warehouse was erected here, and the proprietors, Messrs. Wiley & Çlinard, have handled during the season about sixty thousand pounds, with the expectation, during the next crop season, to increase that amount to several hundred thousand pounds. It is estimated that these two warehouses will handle during the coming season one million pounds, and this estimate is based upon the following data :

" The stimulus given within the last three years to tobacco culture in this section will result in a crop this season of not less than fifteen hundred thousand pounds from the counties of Catawba, Lincoln, Cleaveland, Rutherford, McDowell, Burke, Caldwell, Wilkes, and Iredell. Some of these. counties will continue, more or less, to ship to other markets ; but it is safe to say that out of these Hickory will receive one million pounds, the result of the demand of its factories, which consult their interests by laying in their stocks at home. . . .

" Having given some idea of the increase of production since 1877, I may properly add something about the improvement in quality. In 1877 the great bulk of the crop was poor and trashy to an extent that defied classification. It was an almost valueless nondescript. Every year witnesses improvement, and now sweet fillers and good mahogany wrappers are made as perfectly as can be desired. Many of the new planters have not yet acquired the skill in culture and cure needed to bring out the full perfection of the ' fine gold-leaf ' tobacco which sells at its fabulous prices ; but these same planters have also demonstrated the possibilities of this section for the highest excellence of that beautiful article. . . .

" We shall continue to outstrip those counties (the transmontane region whose specialty is ' bright yellow ') in the production of sweet waxy fillers. . . .

" In regard to prices at Hickory, it is just to our manufacturers to say that a noble public spirit to sustain and build up a home market has led them sometimes to pay for their stocks more than they would have paid in other markets ; at all events paying the prices obtained at distant leading markets with freight charges added. For the fine grades buyers have paid twenty to seventy-five dollars. At these prices it must be admitted that no great margin for speculation is left. These facts should convince our planters that we have a good market, second to no other.

" Our manufacturers will use of the present crop as follows : Hall & Daniel, five hundred thousand pounds; A. W. Marshall, fifty thousand pounds; A. Martin, fifty thousand pounds; H. C. Latta, fifty thousand pounds, and Cobb & Son twenty-five thousand. Other manufacturers will be added to the list before the beginning of the working season of 1881, and it may therefore be safely assumed that the Hickory manufacturers will use in 1881 seven hundred thousand pounds."

WILEY & CLINARD'S WAREHOUSE,

known as "the Farmer's Warehouse," was opened on the 4th of February, 1880. It is a modern building 100x50. It is well constructed and lighted, and has excellent accommodations and conveniences for the planter and his teams. The operations of this house have been given in the preceding statement. Mr. R. J. West is the auctioneer.

FACTORIES.

HALL & DANIEL

are manufacturers of plug, eleven, ten and six inch twist. The estimate of their production, as well as that of other factories in Hickory, is given in the statement of Mr. J. G. Hall.

MARTIN & WARREN

make plug, twist and smoking tobacco, ten inch, sixes and eights plug, and " Hickory " smoking tobacco.

A. W. MARSHALL

makes both plug and smoking, eleven, ten and six inch plug.

H. C. LATTA

manufactures plug and twist, eight inch twist and ten and six inch plug.

COBB & SON

make plug and twist, eleven inch plug and six inch twist.

J. S. TOMLINSON

is the proprietor of the very popular brand " Sweet Sixteen " of smoking tobacco, manufactured for him by A. W. Marshall, which is made of home stock, and commands ready sales, growing steadily in favor.

The character of the tobacco manufactured in Hickory is similar in most respects to that made at Winston.

CLIMATIC INFLUENCES OF THIS SECTION.

Success has invariably attended skill and industry in the cultivation of tobacco in this section. The very considerable number of planters who have come hither from the older counties of Granville, Caswell, and others, are uniform in their testimony that they regard their transfer as an advantageous one ; making tobacco, they think, equally as fine, under certain aids from soil and climate they had not before enjoyed. Mr. R. B. Davis, an old planter from Halifax County, Va., but for a number of years a resident and planter of Catawba County, N. C., in his Manual discusses this question at some length, a few extracts from which are given.

Discussing the difficulties with which the planters of the old counties referred to have to contend, Mr. Davis says:

"Now the planters of Granville (and not of Granville only, but of all the border counties of Virginia and North Carolina) know that it is becoming yearly a thing of increasing difficulty to grow a *ripe and sound crop*. And this for the reason that the plant will not usually stand long enough on the hill to ripen and bleach sufficiently to be easily cured yellow. For, if on the one hand the crop be too long delayed by drought, a fine cure is out of the question ; while on the other hand, if there is rain enough, there is apt to be excess of it ; and then begin all the diseases to which the plant is heir—such as frenching, and firing, and spotting, and rusting, and shedding of the leaves. And with this fear constantly before him, the planter is under the necessity of cutting while the plant is already wasting, but before it is fully and uniformly ripe, giving him, as a result, withered sand lugs at the bottom and green tips at the top, while the middle portion may be such as he desires.

"But in this section of the State the planter is under no such necessity ; for here the plant will stand upon the hill until it has ripened a clear lemon color from top to bottom, without waste, or spot, or blemish. . . . How is this, then, to be accounted for ? The true explanation, I undertake to say, is to be found in the *elevation* of the Piedmont as compared with the central portion of the State. For it is to this greater elevation that we are indebted for our cool nights ; and cool nights, in my opinion, are the salvation of the tobacco crop."

(The elevation of the town of Henderson, in Granville County, is five hundred and five feet above tide-water ; Newton, in Catawba County, is 1021 feet.)

CHAPTER IV.

THE TRANSMONTANE SECTION.

CROSSING the Blue Ridge at the Swannanoa Gap at an elevation of 2657 feet above the sea, a broken plateau spreads out to the limits of the State northwest, west and south, from which spring numerous mountain chains, culminating in the lofty peaks of the Black Mountain, the highest of which is 6707 feet above sea level. There is no level land except narrow strips of valley along the abundant streams. The only lands left to the cultivator are the numerous hills, rising often into the magnitude of mountains, bold and steep, but covered with deep, rich, gray, friable soil, universally clothed, in a state of nature, with a growth of majestic oak, chestnut, walnut, locust, buckeye, maple, black birch (or mahogany), with frequent appearance in ravines of spruce pine and heavy undergrowth of laurel, and frequently of white pine of great height. Rock is not frequent, though sometimes outcropping in the form of cliffs of moderate height, or in veins which stand in vertical strata down the sides of the hills, and occasionally occurring in broad sheets of an acre or more, naked and bare, and asserting a genuine mountain character, which otherwise is contradicted by the luxuriant foliage and giant size of the trees and the richness and beauty of the flowers.

The geological formation is also of the Upper Laurentian. The soil has long been noted for its fertility; producing the cereals in great perfection, and admirably adapted to the grasses. At the time when the turnpike along the French Broad river was the great thoroughfare of travel from the west to east, and when that road was filled with an endless throng of hogs and sheep and cattle driven from the *officina animalium* of East Tennessee and Kentucky, the steep hillsides and tops along the road were cultivated in corn for the supply of the stock on the way to the markets of North and South Carolina. The demand was constant and the business remunerative. But the construction of the railroad lines across the eastern end of Tennessee, connecting with both the northern and southern markets, at the gain both of time and economy, brought the business of the farmer to a sudden end, except as demanded by the necessities of his family. The turnpike became almost as deserted as one of the old Roman Ways, only trod by the tourist or traversed by the weary mail-coach dragging its slow course over a highway torn by freshets and abandoned to decay.

There was little that the farmer could do to better his fortunes, until the fact dawned by slow degrees that these bold and beautiful hills had an adaptability to the production of very fine tobacco almost without equal in the whole State of North Carolina.

Mr. S. C. Shelton, from Henry County, Va., and Mr. W. T. Dickinson, from Pittsylvania County, Va., may justly claim to be the pioneers of tobacco culture in this section, and to have prepared the way by which home markets were at last opened, or by which the fame of Buncombe and Madison tobaccos was wafted to the more distant markets of Lynchburg and Richmond. Of these gentlemen more will be said in its proper connection.

The increased production of tobacco in the county of Buncombe, and the certainty that adjoining counties would speedily engage in the same industry, suggested the enterprise of a

Sales Warehouse

in Asheville, which was undertaken by Mr. J. D. Wilder, of Danville, Va., who had had large experience in the warehouse business with Capt. W. P. Graves, of that town; and in November, 1879, the first warehouse west of the Blue Ridge was opened for the use and encouragement of a home market.

The sales during the season of the current year, 1880, amounted to about six hundred thousand pounds. The supplies were drawn from the four counties of Buncombe, Madison, Haywood aad Yancey. The attention of planters has been turned almost exclusively to the production of brights. Nearly everything sold in this warehouse during the season were wrappers and smokers. Not over one thousand pounds of good fillers were offered. In quality, Mr. Wilder reports that the tobacco is somewhat wanting in body, but surpassingly fine in color. From want of experience, the curing has not been as perfect as it ought to be, nor are the appliances for curing the most approved in kind; and the farmers, from the same want of experience, are deficient in the arts of handling. Sorting is carelessly attended to, and injustice to the finer kinds is done by injudicious intermingling of qualities and colors. But this will be corrected as experience is gained. The average price for the season was from $16 to $17 per hundred; 90 cents a pound was frequently obtained, and for small lots $2.50 per pound has been given.

The mode of curing in common use is with coal or rock flues. In cultivation farmers are beginning to use fertilizers. The lands are fertile, but the seasons are short, and the maturity of the crop is found to be hastened by the aid of artificial manures.

The warehouse of Mr. Wilder is near the Swannanoa Hotel, and is a wooden building 94x64, with sky-light, and ample accommodations for the farmers and their teams.

Of this warehouse Mr. J. D. Wilder is general manager. Mr. J. J. Hill, of Danville, was auctioneer the last season.

Mr. Thomas, of Richmond, Va., is now erecting a large warehouse, which will probably be ready for the incoming crop.

FACTORIES.

Already several of these have come into existence, with results so satisfactory as will lead to the enlargement of their operations and the erection of others. That of

J. E. RAY

has been in operation since 1875, and now obtains all its supplies at home. Its operations are yet somewhat contracted, six or eight hands being employed. Its brands are in high repute—smoking tobacco alone being made. They are "Asheville's Best," made of the best bright leaf, exceedingly beautiful. The next in order is "Black Mountain" and "Swannanoa," both of which are fine grades. Mr. Ray uses some flavoring, principally "deer tongue," obtained from the North Carolina coast counties.

The tobaccos of this factory are gaining repute abroad as well as at home, the greatest demand being from Richmond, Va., and Galveston, Texas.

MR. S. C. SHELTON

is both manufacturer and planter. In the latter capacity he came to Buncombe County from Henry County, Va., with the view of testing the soil and climate of this mountain region. He began his experiments with three acres, with results so satisfactory that he gradually enlarged his operations to one hundred and fifty acres. This, however, he has much reduced, having engaged in manufacture.

He thinks soil and climate both better suited to fine wrappers and smokers, though good fillers can be and are produced in limited supply. The use of fertilizers on fresh lands has not been deemed necessary, but Mr. Shelton approves their use, and this year applied them liberally.

The causes which favor the production of fine tobacco so especially are the elevation of the country, the dryness of the climate by day, and the coolness and moisture of the nights. Tobacco "yellows" on the hill much more readily and uniformly than in the country east of the mountains, and the curing, done by flues or coal, is effected more quickly. The variety planted principally is the broad-leaved Oronoko; the Silky Pryor is the next best. The climate or soil, or both, does not appear to suit the Connecticut seed leaf.

Since Mr. Shelton came to Buncombe the culture of tobacco has rapidly developed, and he thinks it destined to be the finest section in the United States for the finer and fancy qualities. It is becoming the chief industry of the county. Mr. Shelton is the patentee of a new process of curing, which will be spoken of in its proper place.

He took the first premium at the State Fair in 1871 for bright wrappers, and the same at the Virginia State Fair at Richmond in 1872. At the Vienna Exposition he was awarded a silver medal for his brand "Speckled Trout" of manufactured tobacco, and, at the Paris Exposition, had honorable mention for the same brand.

His factory, in Asheville, is engaged in making a favorite brand of twist, put up in very novel and attractive form, and also in the manufacture of superior and much admired smoking tobacco, for which there is already a steady demand.

E. J. HOLMES

began the manufacture of smoking tobacco in Asheville on the 15th of January, 1880. He employs at present eight hands, and makes three brands: " Golden Leaf," which is remarkably beautiful, unequalled in brilliancy of color, and much admired for fine flavor. " Land of the Sky " and " Pisgah " are lower grades, but both of excellent quality. The raw mate rial is bought on the Asheville market. The natural leaf alone is used ; no flavoring whatever being added. These brands are in great demand for the South Carolina and Alabama markets.

Mr. Israel, connected with this factory, prized the first hogshead of tobacco ever shipped from Buncombe County to Danville, in the year 1872.

J. R. Sams intends during the fall to begin the manufacture of smoking tobacco in Asheville.

ARDEN.

One and a half miles from the Henderson County line and ten miles south of Asheville is Arden Park, at which lives Mr. C. W. Beale. He has in operation a cigarette factory, the material for which is obtained in the vicinity. Tobacco is cultivated all around and in the adjoining county of Henderson, and extensive preparations are now being made by clearing the mountain sides to engage largely in the cultivation next year. The country on the south of Asheville contains much gently undulating land, with broader valleys than are found to the north ; these are flanked by mountains of moderate height, and with an inclination gentle enough to invite to cultivation. The soil is darker, with a greater admixture of clay, than the north side of the county. Mr. Beale thinks both climate and soil develop in the tobacco grown here peculiar characteristics of flavor, giving it a marked resemblance to Turkish tobacco. Samples sent to Constantinople have compared favorably with the celebrated Latakia of Asia Minor. This tobacco ripens early, and cures bright with great readiness.

The cigarette factory at this point is the first of its kind west of the mountains, and the peculiar excellence of its product is giving it a wide repute. It was commenced during the year 1880, and is under the management of Mr. James Riley, recently from Buckinghamshire, England.

CHAPTER V.

DOWN THE FRENCH BROAD, BUNCOMBE AND MADISON.

THE road down the French Broad leaves Asheville at some distance from the river, at liberty to divert itself for a while through a country hilly but not mountainous. But the license is soon withdrawn, and four miles from Asheville the road is compelled to come to the river side, and between the broad and boisterous torrent on the one hand and the obtrusive and rugged hills on the other, is glad to compromise for the narrow pass-way left between its rude antagonists. Here and there, at long intervals, the hills retreat far enough to permit the erection of such comfortable mansions as that of General Vance, or such hospitable hostelries as that of Mr. Alexander, or such typical farm-houses as that of Mr. Brown. With these exceptions, there is scarcely room enough between river and mountain for house to stand, until the "Midway House," a mile from Marshall, twenty-one miles from Asheville, is reached.

But because the gorge is narrow and because the hills are bold, it does not follow that nature holds unbroken sway. These hills are covered with deep, rich soil, and crowned with grand forest growth. They are easily brought into cultivation, and respond generously to the demand upon them. Once, as before stated, they were devoted, where cleared, to corn and other grain; now they are coming into more profitable use for tobacco. Occasionally, fine crops are seen almost overhanging the roadside; but it is farther back from the river that the new enterprise is more largely engaged in.

Mr. A. M. Alexander

is one of the largest cultivators along the river. He lives ten miles north of Asheville, at French Broad Post-office; at which point is that delightful summer resort so well known to the eastern tourist. He has been engaged in the culture of tobacco about eight years, increasing his crop each year, and in 1880 having a crop of thirty acres. Crops here are estimated by the acre, not by the number of hills as in the eastern counties.

For bright wrappers Mr. Alexander relies exclusively on new ground. In clearing such the timber is merely deadened, the undergrowth cleared or burnt off, the ground then coultered, then ploughed with a narrow bull tongue, then harrowed and raked, and then the hills are made.

Up to this year he has not used artificial fertilizers. They are now coming into use for lands not fresh. The Star brand and Ober are principally used.

Seed are put in the plant beds in February, and plants set out from the 1st to the 10th of June. Last year Mr. A. planted some as late as the 22d of July, and for the proceeds of that planting received $14 per hundred. He works his tobacco about four times. He tops first to eight leaves, reducing them subsequently to six. More care is being taken with grading than before, and tobacco is now divided into six classes. Curing as a rule is by flues, Ragland's plan being followed.

Worms are quite as abundant here as elsewhere, and the bud-worm is troublesome.

Mr. Alexander's system of farming is to clear his steep hillsides and put them the first year in tobacco. The next year he seeds these down to grass—timothy, orchard and clover—and has now one hundred acres heavily covered. This is not the universal practice. Every farmer now cultivates tobacco, but often uses the same land to the fourth year. The increase this year in the vicinity of French Broad Post-office is about 35 per cent. over last year. Lands have advanced in price, and are valued at from $5 to $10 per acre. 50 cents to $1 an acre not long ago was the general valuation of mountain lands.

The prosperity of the people is rapidly increasing. Tobacco brings money into every household. Last year Mr. Alexander had a female tenant who cultivated two and a half acres with her own hands, and her crop was sold in the Richmond market for $680.

Mr. J. M. Smith

lives in Madison County, immediately across the Buncombe line, and between the waters of the French Broad and Big Ivy. His lands are a continued succession of bold rolling hills, rising to an elevation of from four hundred to five hundred feet above the level of Big Ivy, with absolutely no level ground, the hills rising abruptly from the course of the small streams which intersect them, compelling the use of the hillsides, however steep they may be. The soil is a rich gray loam, with yellowish sandy subsoil. When cleared the land is easily worked, and does not readily wash, owing to the depth and porousness of the superincumbent stratum. Mr. Smith has land in tobacco which he has been cultivating for the fourth year; but he relies for his best results on new ground. These, like Mr. A. M. Alexander, he is seeding to grass, to which he has now devoted about one hundred acres.

He uses fertilizers on the older lands, beginning with the third year. He plants the broad-leaved Oronoko, about five thousand plants to the acre. He has been engaged in tobacco culture since 1870, beginning with fifteen acres, but subsequently reducing his crop until he had acquired experience, and then gradually enlarging until now he has fifty-four acres in cultivation, which, like all the crops seen in this section, were in perfect condition.

Approving the tenant system, he puts it largely into practice, to his advantage and that of his tenant. A tenant was pointed out who came to him the year before last absolutely penniless, but willing to work; telling

Mr. Smith if he would erect him a cabin and put him in charge of a few acres, he would marry and make a crop of tobacco. Mr. Smith built the cabin and assigned him a portion of a ten-acre field sloping abruptly towards the north, and in which the girdled trees were still standing. His first year's crop brought him $650, after paying one-third of the proceeds of sale to his landlord.

This is the country for the poor but industrious man. Mr. Smith has ten tenants who cultivate each from four to ten acres. One tenant last year, from one and a half acres, cured and sold eight hundred and thirty-nine pounds, for which he received $345.94. Another from four and one-quarter acres last year made two thousand nine hundred and eighty pounds, for which he received $985.72; and from the same extent of ground, the year previous, made two thousand eight hundred and ninety-four pounds, for which he was paid $824.20.

In cultivation, Mr. Smith gives one thorough working with the plough and goes through three times with the hoe. He tops to eight leaves as soon as can be done without injury to the top leaves. He cures altogether with reference to wrappers and smokers, using flues, both iron and rock. Coal is not much used.

He plants the last of May or first of June. Tobacco ripens by the first of September, yellowing well on the hill, curing in the barns, which he makes eighteen feet square, with five and a half tiers, being perfected in sixty or seventy hours. He thinks both climate and soil exactly adapted to the fullest development of a superior article of tobacco. The latter contains all the necessary elements; and the former, through the influence of cool nights, and the nightly appearance of fogs, which not only supply moisture but protect against early frost, supplying all the conditions for a perfect plant.

The crop here has no special enemy except the worm, which is not very troublesome. The crop is gone over thoroughly once a week.

The elevation of Mr. Smith's farm is about twenty thousand eight hundred feet above the level of the sea. He finds an eastern or southern exposure the most advantageous.

Mr. Smith and his neighbors sell mostly in the Lynchburg market. The esteem in which the Madison tobacco is held is demonstrated by the following accqunt sales of ten thousand seven hundred and sixty-five pounds sold by Lee, Taylor and Payne, Lynchburg, last winter for Mr. Smith, the original of which is in the possession of the writer of this. The prices paid seem to indicate that all the requisites of color, body, size and perfectness of leaf were fully met:

One lot	54 pounds	at	90	$ 48 60
One "	104 "	"	85	88 40
One "	199 "	"	70	139 30
One "	324 "	"	69	223 56
One "	118 "	"	68	80 24

Three lots	387	pounds	at	· 65	251	55
One "	167	"	"	60	100	20
One "	251	"	"	56	140	56
Two "	605	"	"	55	332	95
Two "	444	"	"	51	226	44
Two "	646	"	"	50	323	00
Two "	272	"	"	49	133	28
One "	414	"	"	48	198	72
One "	345	"	"	47	176	25
One "	399	"	"	46	183	54
Three "	843	"	"	45	389	35
One "	53	"	"	44	23	32
One "	144	"	"	43	61	92
Two "	537	"	"	42	225	54
One "	47	"	"	41	19	27
Five "	1810	"	·"	40	724	00
Two "	333	"	"	38	88	54
One "	26	"	"	37	9	62
One "	300	"	"	36	108	00
Two "	294	"	"	35	102	90
One "	165	"	"	34	56	10
One "	162	"	"	32	51	84
Two "	308	"	"	30	92	40
One "	136	"	"	29	39	44
One "	93	"	"	27	25	11
One "	233	"	"	25	58	25
One "	189	"	"	, 22½	42	52
One "	60	"	"	21½	12	90
One "	373	"	"	20	74	60
	10,765				$4852	21

Or an average of over $45.00 per hundred.

W. T. DICKINSON

lives in Buncombe County, near Weaversville, ten miles northeast of ·Asheville, and is largely engaged in the culture of tobacco. He is one of the most experienced farmers in the county, having acquired his knowledge in Pittsylvania County, Va., from which he removed to Buncombe in 1854. He is therefore fully competent to form an accurate judgment upon the quality of the mountain tobacco. His crop this year is forty-four acres, of which thirty-two are in one body.

His lands are gray, with red clay subsoil, soil much broken and heavily timbered. Planting is done late in May or early in June, and the plants grow off readily, yellowing finely in the field, and ready for cutting early in September.

From the ease with which curing is effected, Mr. Dickinson thinks both soil and climate peculiarly adapted to fine tobacco. He thinks it matures earlier than in Virginia, through the influence of cool nights and heavy dews. In curing he uses the ordinary sheet-iron flues. The time of curing is shortened by the maturity of the leaf as it comes from the fields. He uses fertilizers, the Anchor brand, on all his lands, old and new, with a product of about twelve hundred pounds to the acre.

The cultivation is rapidly extending. Yellow tobacco is almost the sole object. The lands, which are cheap and abundant, and held at an average of five dollars per acre, are taken up by the citizens of the vicinity, and, as yet, there is little immigration into this part of the county.

Mr. Dickinson sells partly in Danville, partly in Lynchburg, and obtains good prices. His last year's crop is still on hand.

He describes the lands in Yancey County, adjoining Buncombe and Madison, as identical in character, and coming rapidly into use for the same purposes. In all these counties he estimates the increase of the crop of this year over that of the last at from one hundred to three hundred per cent.

Marshall and Vicinity.

Marshall, the county seat of Madison County, is compressed into one of those narrow recesses which rarely open in this part of the French Broad, the open ground being not more than eighty yards wide and extending about four hundred yards along the river. A small island in front once formed part of the town, but was overflowed in the great flood of 1877, and has now reverted to nature. Back of the steep and toppling hills which overhang the town lies a country broken and mountainous indeed, but very fertile. These are reached from the river through the narrow gorges which occasionally divide the hills, and furnish roadways roughly available for vehicles. These furnish the roads to market.

Since the discovery of the capacity of the lands for the production of fine tobacco, they have come rapidly into use.

The superior fertility of the Madison County lands makes itself known to the most careless observation. The great size of the trees, their greater variety, the luxuriousness of foliage, and the density of the undergrowth, all indicate wonderful exuberance of soil, increasing in richness with the descent of the French Broad; and Madison County may justly claim to possess advantages surpassed by no other, if equalled by any county.

The course of the French Broad is generally north. All the lands on the east side are finely adapted to tobacco, those on the west largely so, but to less extent. The culture within the past three years has become a part of the business of almost every farmer. The increase this year in acreage is about fifty per cent.

In the infancy of a great industry its pioneers deserve honorable mention, and the names of some of the farmers within a radius of five miles of Marshall are given.

Wallace Rollins adopts the tenant system, and has this year one hundred acres in cultivation; I. Nichols has 30 acres; H. Rice, 28 acres; James M. Gudger, 27 acres; H. A. White, 25 acres; P. H. Kilpatrick, 20 acres; M. A. Robinson, 20 acres; Z. Henderson, 15 acres; J. M. Robinson, 15 acres.

At Mars Hill, ten miles north of Marshall, H. J. Carter, S. C. Huff, I. R. Sams, and E. Carter, average about fifteen acres each.

Last year Z. Henderson, from two and three-quarter acres, netted $1027; Lee Henderson, from one hundred and forty rods, sold four hundred and fifty pounds at 75 cents per pound; renters from fifty acres averaged $212 per acre.

Morning fogs along the river are of almost daily and nightly occurrence, with the singular exception of the area embracing the Warm Springs, sixteen miles below Marshall, which is said never to be obscured by fog. This may be the result of the thermal influences, which give heat to the Warm Springs and which equalize temperature. These fogs are considered highly advantageous to tobacco in giving moisture and in retarding frosts. The season of maturity being prolonged, that for planting may be postponed. Last year Z. Roberts planted on the 29th of June and obtained an average of $30 for his crop, making seven hundred and fifty pounds to the acre. Geo. Gohagan planted late. In ninety days from planting his crop was cut, for which he was paid, at the barn, $25 for the crop, round.

The average per acre throughout Madison and Buncombe is estimated at seven hundred and fifty to eight hundred pounds.

MARKETS.

Most of the tobacco of the county is carried off to Richmond, Lynchburg, and some to Danville. A fair proportion is sold at home. Mr. D. F. Davis, merchant at Marshall, is a considerable handler, having taken last year direct from the farmers about sixty thousand pounds, acting as their agent, and he finds from the number of sellers that nearly every farmer in the county to a greater or less extent raises tobacco.

THE WAREHOUSE

of C. A. Nichols & Co., however, affords the largest facilities for the home market. It is a wooden building of ample size and good arrangement, with daily sales in proper season.

From a report of sales made January 26th, 1880, it appears that during the preceding fortnight sales of 6,194 pounds were made for $2,041.25, being an average of $33.00 per hundred; a very high average, and one seldom exceeded. The business of this warehouse during the coming season is expected vastly to increase, both on account of the good prices obtained there and the very large increase of production in the surrounding country.

In addition to the counties west of the mountains already named as engaged in the culture of tobacco, very encouraging progress has been made in Haywood, which possesses equal excellencies of soil and climate. During this season many very considerable crops have been planted, and are reported in good condition. Transylvania County, equally favored by nature, has undertaken the culture, and so have some of the counties west of Haywood. The whole country west of the mountains, at all adapted to tillage, may be expected to strive after the same prize that is enriching the others.

CHAPTER VI.

IT thus appears from the preceding statements that a new and very large territory is added to the production of that beautiful substance, fine yellow tobacco, which, confined hitherto to somewhat well defined limits, has commanded prices which might almost appear fabulous or fanciful had they not been sustained by healthy and unwavering demand. The question may arise whether, with greatly increased supply, prices will not necessarily be reduced. This undoubtedly will be the case inevitably were the demand confined to the United States, which, until within a few years, and for special uses, has been the sole consumer. But within those few years Europe has become somewhat familiar with the merits of bright yellow tobacco. One of the beneficent results of the Philadelphia Exposition was to bring the world together ; to bring its peoples into close contact, and present their varied industries and products to comparison or contrast. The bright yellow tobacco was favorably made known, almost for the first time, to England and France. The former has become a consumer to a considerable and growing extent, the exports having increased within two years four or five-fold. But for the antiquated restrictions imposed under the Continental regie system, the French, a nation of smokers, and constitutionally nice and delicate in taste, would also become large consumers. Italy and Austria also would be glad to exchange their heavy nicotized native leaf for the fragrant and innocent weed of North Carolina.

International législation should be invoked to destroy a system which carries with it the ignorance of political economy which characterized the dark ages, and banish from the commercial code modes fashioned on the principles of monopolies, the rewards of venal favorites, or the desperate resorts of impoverished monarchs.

But the high prices obtained of late years must of necessity give way to some extent before the excess of supply over a demand abroad dependent upon future creation.

The American people lie under the grievous error that they are the principal producers of tobacco, and that, as with cotton, the whole world is tributary to them. Hence they are impatient under the fluctuations of the market, ascribing them to the combinations among dealers by which prices are regulated by interested caprice. It is well that Americans should know that tobaccco is the production of almost every country on the globe; that its flexibility exceeds that of almost any other agricultural product; that it ranges from the equator to from 40 to 45 degrees on either side; that it is of universal consumption; and that therefore, as a foreign product, American tobacco can enter upon the markets of Europe in successful competition only by some incontestible excellencies of quality and with some favorable conditions of price.

The total crop of the United States for the four years ending in 1874 was 1,775,000,000 pounds; the total exports abroad for the same period were 982,697,476 pounds. Now, the United States come into competition with the following countries, whose products are given for the year 1874:

The German Empire produced 99,516,501 lbs., Hungary 45,000,000, the average price of which was 3s. 6d., the tobacco being bright, and used for cigars and cutting. The Austrian Empire, including Hungary, produced 58,000,000 lbs. Turkey produced 43,000,000 lbs. of light yellow tobacco, used for cigars and cutting, the best coming from Macedonia and Syria. The prices varied from 3d. to from 3s. to 4s. There were no exports to the United States, all being to other parts of Europe. North Brazil produçes a tobacco used for cigars and cutting, at a price from 3d. to 1s. 6d. The exports from Bahia, which were mainly to England, France, Germany and Holland, were, in 1869, 19,914.523 lbs.; in 1870. 23,864,909 lbs.; in 1873, 34,419,385. The export duty is 9 per cent. imperial and 6 per cent. provincial. Cuba produces exclusively cigar tobacco, at prices ranging from 1s. to 12s. A Cuba plantation consists of thirty-three acres, and produces 9,000 lbs. The Philippine Islands produce 23,000,000 lbs, one-half of which is exported to Europe, at prices from 6d. to 5s. The business is a government monopoly. Japan of late years has largely increased its production, which is a light brown leaf, used for cutting, and sold at from 3d. to 8d. The plant is not cut like American, but pulled at intervals. It is largely used by English manufacturers when American is high. China produces a large quantity of light brown and bright yellow, mostly consumed at home, except when exported under the stimulus of high prices abroad. Prices range from 3d. to 6d. New Grenada produces a cigar tobacco valued at 6d. to 2s.; exports in 1868-9, 12,571,805 lbs. Java exports 33,000,000 lbs. light cutting and cigar tobacco, valued at 8d. to 4s.—all to Holland. Ecuador exports 1,120,000 of light cigar wrappers, worth 1s. to 2s. Venezuela, Guayaquil and Guatemala export to Germany and England about 4,000,000 lbs. of a poor, light cigar tobacco which burns badly. Mexico produces a light quality, suitable for cigars, to the extent of 6,000,000 lbs., at a price of from 8d. to 1s. 6d. The business is subject to government restrictions. Tobasco produces a tobacco equal to Cuba, but the amount is not accurately known. Porto Rico produces a small, light tobacco worth 6d.; the exports in 1871 were 1,489,490 lbs. to Germany and 206,000 to England. San Domingo produces a large, light tobacco valued at 6d. to 1s. 6d.; the crop is estimated at 8,960,000 lbs., which is evidently too little. Jamaica produces a small crop, similar in quality to Cuba. Greece produces a light yellow cutting tobacco, at a valuation of from 3d. to 4d., exporting in 1873, 339,712 lbs., mostly to Great Britain. France produced from 1854 to 1868, inclusive, 45,843,920. The control of tobacco in France is a monopoly, as will be elsewhere noticed. Russia raises, mostly in the Crimea, about 23,000,000 lbs., a tobacco resembling American brights, mahoganies and blacks, which is air cured. None is exported, and there is an import demand. British India produces large crops of both light and heavy tobacco, mostly common cutting, and worth only from 1½d. to 3d.; but earnest efforts are being made to improve the quality. Australia produces a coarse tobacco, suitable for plug fillers, which is protected by a duty of 25 per cent. on manufactured tobacco and 15 per cent. on leaf. The quality of the product is improving. The yield is 1300 lbs. per acre. In New South Wales the product is 976 per acre, in Tasmania 2016 per acre. In Melbourne 112 shillings has been obtained per ton for good colonial leaf; but good is rare, owing to difficulty of curing. Spain produces largely a coarse tobacco. The import is a government monopoly.

It will thus be seen that nearly every nation under the sun is a producer of tobacco, and that all, or nearly all, seek a European market. The United States thus find themselves faced by a universal competition. Nor is this all. High duties in Great Britain and Germany and government monopolies in France, Austria, Spain and Italy, close the gates to only such amount of imports as it is the pleasure of those governments to admit. To aggravate their disadvantages, the Americans persist in the production of low grades, throwing everything, good or bad, on the market, overstocking it, and keeping alive, as stock on hand, thousands of hogsheads which it would be wise economy to destroy, but whose existence excuses holders in pleading in justification of low prices an excess of supply over demand.

The Report of the Commissioner of Agriculture for 1878 says: " The fact is, that in 1869, the crop of the United States amounted to but 324 million pounds against, in round numbers, 424 millions in 1870, 410 millions in 1871; 505 millions in 1872, 502 millions in 1873, 358 millions in 1874, 520 millions in 1875, 482 millions in 1876, and 581 millions in 1877, until the planters have gone on, year by year, increasing the crop, until they have glutted the markets of the world. . . . Over-production—that is, the production of *poor* tobacco—is the controlling . cause of the unhappy condition in which the tobacco planters of the United States now find themselves."

And again: "The production of *good* tobacco, of whatever kind, has never been too large. It is the production of poor tobacco that has caused the mischief. Like every other farm product of poor quality, whether poor cotton, poor rice, poor wheat or poor corn, poor tobacco has a weary way to travel to find a purchaser. . . . In Liverpool, Bremen, New Orleans, Baltimore and New York alone, the stock had accumulated Nov. 1, 1878, (and the proportion is kept up to this day) to 159,761 hhds. against 89,606 hhds. for the same day of 1875."

The whole question is summed up in the following sensible conclusion:

" 1. That over-production, the production at all of low grade tobacco, will always result in low prices for the entire commodity.

" 2. That the planters of the United States have the remedy in their own hands, that remedy being the reduction of area ; this reduction to result, from increased attention to cultivation and cure, in largely increased crops, to be sold at greatly enhanced prices.

" In a word, one acre must be made to yield what it has hitherto taken two or three to produce ; and this quantity must be made immeasurably superior in quality to that grown on the greater number of acres.

" *The whole world wants good tobacco, and will pay for it. Scarcely any people on earth wants poor tobacco, or will pay for it at any price.*"

CHAPTER VII.

THE GREAT CENTRAL BELT.

BY far the most important tobacco region of the State is that which is near its geographical centre. It is in this that this crop has been the great staple for several generations. It is here that the greatest experience has been acquired; and it is here that, in certain grades, the very highest excellence has been attained. This region embraces the counties of Warren, Granville, Orange, Alamance, Person, Caswell, and Rockingham, and portions of Chatham and Guilford. Most of it lies in the Laurentian formation, in which is included the light gray lands known as "chinquepin land," which has been found so suitable to the perfect production of "bright yellow tobacco." Other portions of it are embraced in the Huronian system, in which are produced the darker tobaccos suitable for fillers and mahogany or dark wrappers. The whole surface of this region is generally gently undulating, but occasionally broken by lines of bold, steep hills. The soil was originally covered with a growth of many varieties of oak, hickory, poplar, walnut, maple and pine, with heavy undergrowth of dogwood, chinquepin, sour wood, and other shrubby trees.

Tobacco culture has been, in most parts of these counties, the industry of generations; and skill, become hereditary in white and black farmers, has given the production a character for excellence which is sustained in every market, and which is equally prominent in both the lighter and darker qualities. Hence the markets dependent upon these counties can obtain supplies of whatever grade that is desirable, giving them, when the claim of North Carolina to an independent position in relation to the tobacco trade is recognized, a pre-eminence of choice over almost all others.

The wasteful habits of past generations, in possession of abundant labor needing constant employment, and owning unlimited bodies of forest land inviting to clearance, has long since exhausted the virgin freshness of the soil. "New grounds" are rarely to be had, second growth lands become their substitute; but when these do not occur, recourse must be had to artificial fertilizers. These are universally relied upon as indispensable to the production of "bright yellow" on lands not absolutely fresh. They are effective in imparting vitality to the still unexhausted original elements of the soil, and giving the tobacco of this section a character which is the wonder of the agricultural chemist, as well as the envy of less fortunate rivals.

The yellow tobacco familiar on the Durham, Danville and other large markets, and the material of the famous brands of Blackwell & Co. and others, was analyzed by the celebrated agricultural chemist, Dr. Augustus

Voelcker, of London,* at the instance of Mr. John Ott, of Richmond, Va. It was classed as "Granville Bright," but is the same tobacco used by Blackwell and others.

The following is the composition of the mineral portion (ash):

Lime	23.39
Magnesia	4.05
Oxide of Iron.	.81
Potash	18.55
Chloride of Potassium	5.82
Chloride of Sodium	7.17
Phosphoric Acid	3.36
Sulphuric Acid	3.37
Soluble Silica.	13.80
Fine Sand	5.72
Carbonic Acid and Moss	13.96
	100.00

Deducting sand and carbonic acid, and the composition of the pure tobacco is as follows:

Lime	29.12
Magnesia	5.04
Oxide of Iron	1.01
Potash	23.09
Chloride of Potassium	7.25
Chloride of Sodium	8.93
Phosphoric Acid	4.18
Sulphuric Acid	4.19
Soluble Silica	17.19
	100.00

And the following is Dr. Voelcker's analysis of the detailed composition of "fancy brights":

Moisture		14.68
†Gum, or extractive matter, soluble in water		36.17
Mineral matter		8.92
Nicotine		1.37
Resinous compounds, oil and other constituents soluble in ether and alcohol		6.68
‡ { Digestible woody fibre	14.43	
Indigestible woody fibre	12.42	32.18
Mineral matter, insoluble in water	4.33	
		100.00

* Chemist of the Royal Agricultural Society.   † Containing nitrogen.
‡ Nitrogen of portion insoluble in water.

Dr. Voelcker, commenting upon the foregoing analysis, says :

" I find merely traces of nitrates in the 'fancy bright tobaccos,' which, perhaps, is one of the reasons why the tobacco has a very mild taste ; for in all biting and strong tobacco I find the nitrates present in very considerable quantities." And again he says : "Another and most important fact which my investigations have brought to light is that the Granville County tobacco which you (Mr. Ott) sent me contains *little nicotine,* which I am inclined to regard as a good feature in this tobacco. The coarse, strong tobacco such as grown in the Palatinate, and some of the coarse, highly manured Virginia tobacco, contain three or four times as much nicotine." (Note—the strongest Virginia and Kentucky tobacco contains from 6 to 7 per cent. of nicotine.) And Dr. Voelcker adds : " 'Granville Bright' is one of the finest flavored mild tobaccos I ever smoked ; poor in nicotine and albuminous compounds, the absence of which is a good and distinguishing character. Albuminous and nitrogenous compounds, when largely present, give off the odor of singed feathers or burnt bone."

It will be noted that Dr. Voelcker uses the term " Granville Bright " as a general name, in the absence of any classification for North Carolina tobacco. It is almost the same as the bright yellow of the whole State, that of the west varying slightly in composition, and should be recognized on the markets of the world by the rightful and distinctive classification of NORTH CAROLINA BRIGHTS. Its identity and its origin are concealed under the deceptive and unmeaning misnomer of *Virginia Strips !*

While these bright yellow tobaccos are the distinctive feature of the products of this Great Central Belt, the aim and ambition of all planters to produce, and the great source of reward for their labors, the great variety of soils in this belt offers inducement to the equal perfection of the richer and darker qualities suitable for chewing, little inferior to the best leaf of the favored counties of Virginia, which is undoubtedly, for its purpose, the best in the world. Hence, in Durham, in Henderson, in Oxford, and in Danville, Va., which is largely dependent on this North Carolina " Middle Belt," the manufacturer at home, the buyer on orders, or the contractor for foreign governments, can on any one market make his selections, his orders, his contracts complete, in *North Carolina warehouses, of North Carolina tobacco.* It is a wrong, it is an injustice, for which North Carolinians themselves are mainly responsible through their ignorance of the extent of their resources, or apathy in asserting their power, or ignoble deference to the influence of an accepted classification. Is it right that a State, which this year will produce fifty million of pounds of tobacco ; which for some years has fallen not very far short of this amount ; which produces almost exclusively one variety, the best of its kind in the world, and abundantly of other grades which Virginia is not ashamed to adopt as her own, should go abroad under the protecting shadow of another name, and seek sale and favor under the patronage of a false classification ?

In a review of this middle belt it is not proposed, as in the western section, to note the operations of individual planters. In the latter section the business is new, and the pioneers in it are readily designated. In the other, it is the universal avocation of whole counties, and the individuals far too numerous for specification. But information will be given of the most important manufacturing and sales points, such as will illustrate the magnitude of an industry which animates the town and the country alike, which invigorates agricultural life, and gives vigor to the energies of commerce and manufactures; and which, in addition, gives North Carolina a powerful motive and occasion to assert and maintain a commercial autonomy, merged, in the past, in the life of a venerated sister State.

CHAPTER VIII.

MARKETS OF THIS SECTION.

IN the centre and along the margins of this belt are markets, sprung into existence by a demand for their agency, and operating as an active stimulus to the larger expansion of tobacco culture. Danville, in Virginia, and Milton, in North Carolina, were established markets, in minor degree, before the war; Durham and Reidsville, in North Carolina, have been called into being by the trade in tobacco, while Hillsboro, Henderson, and Oxford have enlarged greatly their original means of prosperity by adding this to their other branches of business.

The market in North Carolina which has made the most rapid development and attracted a large share of attention is

DURHAM,

in Orange County. It is situated on the North Carolina Railroad, twenty-five miles west of Raleigh, the capital of North Carolina. Designated originally as a railroad station, and known at first only for its connection with the State University, for which it was the point of transfer, it lingered in undisturbed obscurity until the chance operations of the latter days of the war gave it notoriety as the halting-place of the victorious army of Sherman in its pursuit of the retreating Johnson; halted, that negotiations for peace might be entered into between the chiefs of the hostile armies. These negotiations ended in terms honorable to Sherman and favorable to the ruined South; terms, unfortunately for the wellbeing of the whole country, not endorsed by the Government at Washington, and postponing for many a long and miserable year that pacification for which the South earnestly and honestly longed.

This halt of Sherman's army was fruitful of unlooked-for consequences upon the destiny of Durham. The soldiery, idle in their camps and oppressed by the sudden contrast of active hostility and indolent inaction, sought relief in such solace as accident might present. The little tobacco factory of J. R. Green had wafted its cheer through the war among the comfortless and half-starved ranks of the Confederate army. There was no more welcome visitor from home than a present of Green's tobacco, and sisters and sweethearts made it a pious and a pleasant duty to express their affection through these little mementos, decorated with all the skill which taste or affection might suggest. The Federal army struck at its fountain-head the source of the cheer which lightened the hours of the weary Confederate. Durham proved no Capua to it; but it made impressions and it begat tastes which became ineradicable. Durham Smoking Tobacco became a national necessity. The returned and disbanded soldiery turned wistful and longing eyes back to the scene which had relieved the monotony of peaceful camp-life by its grateful and luxurious resources, and impatient hands were stretched out from every part of the American Union for a modicum of the fragrant compound. The effect on the fortunes of Durham was immediate and surprising. Factories sprang rapidly into existence, warehouses were established, population flocked in, a town grew up around the once obscure station, and now Durham is known throughout the wide world wherever the grateful incense of its tobacco ascends. Its six warehouses sell annually from ten to twelve million pounds of the planter's tobacco. Its ten or twelve factories manufacture from four to six million pounds of a fabric which finds its way to every part of the habitable globe. The population, the real growth of the last six years, has now reached 3,600, and continuously increases. And if, as it may be hoped when the magnitude of the tobacco interests of North Carolina are acknowledged, the State is recognized as a commercial factor in the great transactions incident to the traffic, then Durham must hold a more commanding position than it even now possesses.

The different business establishments will be noted in detail, beginning with the warehouses.

WAREHOUSES.

REAMS' WAREHOUSE.

In connection with the warehouse business of Durham, it is proper to ascribe to H. A. Reams the honor of pioneership in the business. He sold the first leaf ever sold at auction in Durham, on the 18th day of May, 1871. His first sale was in a small factory building, in which he continued until the fall of 1872; the business having increased so rapidly, much larger floor capacity was required, and in that year he opened in a warehouse building erected by W. T. Blackwell & Co., in which he continued until the fall of 1877 ; in that year he erected his present warehouse, a building 40x175 feet, on one of the most elegible lots in the town, being in its centre on Main street, and near the depot. In 1879 his trade had so largely increased that he was compelled to enlarge his buildings to double their former capacity, giving them now a floorage capacity of 14,000 feet of salesroom, with a basement of the same size. The warehouse is lit by 32 skylights, containing sixty-four 10x20 glass to each skylight, making 2,048 square feet of light, with 435 feet of shelter for wagons; making the whole warehouse one of the largest and best arranged in North Carolina.

Mr. Reams has sold up to this time some thirty million pounds of tobacco, and his large yearly averages are well sustained.

PARRISH & BLACKWELL

are the successors of E. J. Parrish, who presents one of the most remarkable instances of successful enterprise in a town where all is life and energy. He commenced the tobacco business in 1871 as auctioneer, in the first tobacco warehouse established in Durham, and continued as such until 1873, when he became proprietor of the new warehouse just finished, and known as "The Farmer's." In 1876 he was the successful bidder for the "Durham Warehouse," which he occupied at an annual rental of $2,000 for three years, and his business increased rapidly; and in 1879 he erected the present fine building, occupied now by the firm of Parrish and Blackwell, at a cost of $32,000, and which is confessedly the best structure of its kind in North Carolina. It is of brick, 56x225 feet, with a deep and commodious basement used for storage, and with apartments for farmers. The roof is a suspension structure, pierced along its whole length by four rows of solid glass skylights. Along the sides run covered sheds the whole length of the building, on one side 225x16, and on the other 225x10, with a park-shed 41x150, with two rows of skylights, large enough to hold one hundred wagons. Elegantly appointed offices give pleasant places of business to the eight or ten young men necessary for the duties of the house ; these offices, like all other parts of the building, being lighted with gas.

The opening day of the house, September 29th, 1879, was a prominent one in the annals of Durham, many hundred farmers with their wagons loaded with the tobacco of the adjoining counties congregating to take advantage of the animation of the auspicious day. Upwards of 80,000 pounds were sold at this warehouse on that day, for an aggregate sum of $15,000; and the happy fortune of so favorable a beginning has never deserted the house. Mr. J. W. Blackwell was admitted as a partner in the business of Mr. Parrish in April, 1880 ; and under the firm name of Parrish & Blackwell, the house continues to enlarge in its operations, and claims, and with reason, to transact a larger amount of business than any similar house in North Carolina, and has established a national reputation among the leaf-tobacco markets of the country for the uniformity of its classification and the honesty of its prizing and other essentials to good repute.

FARMER'S WAREHOUSE

was originally "Parrish's Warehouse." In 1876 it was taken charge of by Walker, Lyon & Co. In 1879 a change was made and the firm is now known as Walker & Burton. The warehouse is of wood, 40x150. Receipts are from the adjoining counties, together with large quantities of shipped tobacco. Receipts include all varieties.

WILKERSON BROS. WAREHOUSE

was opened January, 1880, by J. C. and J. M. Wilkerson. The building is of wood, 140x40, with good skylight, and ample yard accommodations.

Sales are had daily, C. W. A. Barham auctioneer. The supplies have been mostly from Orange, Caswell, Person, and Granville counties in North Carolina.

In regard to the crop ot 1880, the senior member of this firm, a very experienced tobacconist in all branches of the avocation, reports that in quantity the crop is an average one, but in quality inferior, owing to wet weather in August. The cure of fine bright was made with difficulty. The crop was cut about the usual time. Bright and smokers predominate, including nice bright wrappers, nice bright cutters, bright fillers and bright smokers. There is little sun-cured and little dark, the aim of planters being brights exclusively.

Recently, this house has withdrawn from the handling of farmer's tobacco, devoting itself exclusively to the sales of package tobacco.

The Banner Warehouse

was opened April 9th, 1879, by Lea, Corbett & Co. In 1880 the firm name of the house was changed to Lea Bros., Mr. Corbett going out, and Messrs. W. A. and J. T. Lea succeeding to the business. The warehouse is of wood, 40x175, with extensive lots for teams and wagons. Their sales take place daily. J. Q. A. Barham is auctioneer. The supplies are from Alamance, Orange, Caswell, Person, and Granville. The character of the tobacco includes all grades of bright wrappers and smokers, with a proportionate supply of fillers.

The Planter's Warehouse

was opened by Stokes & Thomas in 1874, who continued business for a year, and then sold their interest to W. A. Wahab & Co. They continued in business for three or four years, and in the fall of 1878 sold to Cooper, Blackwell & Co., who in turn were succeeded in February, 1880, by Cooper & Lunsford.

The warehouse is of wood, 174x50, with a commodious basement 50x150, with ample shed-rooms and fine lots for wagons and teams.

The proprietors are L. E. Cooper of Granville County, and Jos. G. Lunsford of Person County. C. E. Crabtree is principal clerk, W. H Osborne of Granville auctioneer, and John W. Pope of Orange floor manager.

The sales for the past year were large and show progressive increase, and embrace supplies from all adjacent counties, from Virginia, and from the new producing counties of western North Carolina.

The total sales of the warehouses in Durham during the season of 1880 are estimated at twelve million pounds, a large majority of which was farmer's tobacco sold from the wagons. A larger quantity of package tobacco than usual was received from other markets. The characteristic excellence of the higher grades of smoking tobacco has been maintained by the purchase of the tobaccos of the adjacent counties, which possess peculiar qualities, as shown by analysis elsewhere quoted.

The quantity manufactured was about four and a half millions, producing a revenue for the year ending September 1st, 1880, of $726,641.90.

FACTORIES.

W. T. Blackwell & Co.

This house has no merely local name. It is known the wide world over, as familiar and as welcomed in the antipodes as in the little town to which it gave impetus and fame. For the fortunes of Durham and Blackwell & Co. are one and inseparable; as one has expanded in business, so has the other enlarged and flourished. And while other and prospering houses have achieved fortune and reputation in the same pursuit, it is no disparagement to them to assign to Blackwell & Co. the undisputed pre-eminence in magnitude of operations and widespread diversity of market and demand. And this house has so grown up to its dimensions that each successive step of progress may be traced by the contemporaneous eye. Within a few steps of the present large factory is to be seen the little wooden building, with somewhat pretentious front, which, within the past decade, sufficed the wants of the proprietors; that, in turn, giving way to the large brick edifice, five years ago thought the creation of a vain ambition; it in turn subjected to the large additions which dwarfed all previous effort, possibly not yet filling the measure which continual growth of business may exact.

Reference has been made elsewhere to the origin of the demand for Durham smoking tobacco, of which Mr. J. R. Green sagaciously took advantage, increasing his facilities for manufacturing, and adopting a distinguishing brand and device, making the "Durham Bull" thenceforth immortal.

It was in 1868 that W. T. Blackwell and J. R. Day, then tobacco jobbers, bought a half interest in the business of J. R. Green; and this partnership was continued until the death of Mr. Green, which took place the next year, when the other partners purchased his interest from the heirs. In 1870, Mr. Julian S. Carr, of Chapel Hill, N. C., bought a third interest in the business. In 1878 Mr. J. R. Day sold his share to the other partners, and the present firm name was assumed.

To the long and vexatious, but finally triumphant litigation by which the right to the undisputed use of the "Durham Bull" brand was established, reference can only be made. It is sufficient to say that the settlement of controversy removed the barriers to that expansion of operations forced by the spread of well-earned reputation.

About five years ago the nucleus of the present large structure was erected. It was a brick building, four stories high, and one hundred feet square, of fair architectural claims, and a striking object, with its many windows adorned with cream-colored mouldings, contrasting well with the red brick of the walls ; with its rich, deep cornice, and with the large panel over the central entrance, on which was emblazoned in colossal proportions the typical idea of the business—the great Durham Bull, rampant and triumphant.

Last year, enlargements became imperative ; and additions were made which now give a building with a north frontage of two hundred feet, with a height of four stories ; with two wings of the same height extending back one hundred and sixty feet. Mr. Blackwell himself supervised the whole work of enlargement. He designed all the interior arrangements, rigidly inspected every piece of timber that went into the structure, and scrutinized almost every brick that was laid ; and this intelligent and watchful supervision pervades every operation of the firm.

The interior is systematically apportioned to the many and varied operations. On the first floor are the elegantly furnished offices for the clerical force, and also for the heads of the house. On the same floor is the

Shipping Room,

to which are brought the packages after they have been filled and stamped, to be marked for their destination, whether it be to New York or Galveston, to Boston or San Francisco, to Quebec or Rio de Janeiro, to Liverpool or Berlin, to Melbourne or Hokodadi—for it goes to all these places and many besides ; and more than six hundred boxes, representing 17,000 pounds, are daily borne from this room to the railroad depot near by, by files of negro porters, in merry and picturesque despatch. These packages are partly of wood, partly of paper encased in canvas ; and there is also a full supply of handsome tin cases to be used for special purposes.

The Stamping Room

is immediately above the shipping room, and is 90x120 feet. Here ninety persons are busily at work stamping and casing the little packages which are brought in from the packing room. The celerity and dexterity in handling and affixing the stamps, a work done principally by small negro boys, is somewhat marvellous. There are ten stamping tables, the stamps running from eighths to pounds. The cancelling room, the room also from which stamps are delivered, is separate from but connected with the stamping room. The monthly average of stamps used by this firm is in value about $45,000.

The Packing Room,

above the stamping room, is of the same size. Here about seventy hands are employed, filling the sacks by means of presses worked by steam, which is the motive-power for all the operations of the factory, the engine being in a remote part of the building, power being communicated by shafts and belts. Each of these presses is attended by five persons, who weigh, feed, fill, tie and case with remarkable rapidity and accuracy. There are now thirteen of these presses in use. The bags are no small item of expense. They are made by contract with parties in Durham, who in the aggregate furnish a daily supply of from 70,000 to 80,000, representing a monthly consumption of cotton cloth amounting to 92,000 yards.

Connected with this room is the Flavoring Department, where an important part of the series of processes by which the tobacco of Blackwell & Co. has acquired its character is performed. Eighty gallons of rum are daily used in flavoring, and ten thousand pounds of tonqua beans are required; supplemented by the "deer tongue," a native of the county of New Hanover, N. C., with a very delicate vanilla-like aroma.

The Manufacture

in all its processes is too familiar to be detailed in full. It is sufficient to say that the raw leaf, which is selected and graded with the utmost care, is stored in the drying-room in the fourth story, where it is spread on lattice shelves, and heated to dryness by steam pipes. This makes the tobacco very friable. When wanted, the dried leaf is passed by the shute to the ground floor, to a room in which six or eight cutting machines, similar in construction to wheat-threshers, reduce it to fragments. From the cutting machines, the tobacco, leaf, dust, stems and all, goes to the basement below, and is then carried by "elevators" to the third story, where it falls upon sieves by which the stems are removed. The residuum, granulated tobacco, pieces of leaf and dust, is then passed by automatic machinery to the floor below and "bolted," and the granulated tobacco comes out pure and clean, ready for the final operation of flavoring. The dust is bagged and shipped to the North as a component of fertilizers.

, The granulated tobacco is stored in the upper floors, where it lies in huge embankments awaiting transfer.

Under the roof, throughout the building, are a series of iron tanks, each holding one thousand gallons of water, filled by steam power operating through a length of two hundred and fifty yards of pipe, elevating the water to a height of seventy-five feet. Connected with each tank is a hose pipe, conveniently coiled upon the upright supports of the roof, with all the appliances for immediate use close at hand, so that on an alarm of fire the whole could be instantly flooded. Barrels filled with water also stand ready in every room.

The western extension of the building is used for several purposes. One large room is used for the storage of empty boxes. Another is now used for the manufacture of

Cigarettes,

a newly introduced branch of this business. The room devoted to this is 110x45 feet, and 82 hands are now employed. Work was begun in August,

1880, and the first shipment was made on the first of September; and the demand at once exceeded the supply. The stock used is very superior, and the cigarettes are put up in very tasteful packages.

"Long Cut"

is also a new industry of this factory, and the quality of the article made is excellent. It is made of the best bright cutters, and like all the stock used in the factory, is bought on the Durham market.

Blackwell & Co.'s establishment is complete in itself. It has its work-shops of wood and iron where machinery is made or repaired; it has its saw mill and planing machines where all its immense supply of boxes is made, using for them 75,000 feet per month; it has its paper box factory to supply its fancy work; it has its printing office to print its myriads of labels, posters, circulars, etc.; and it has its army of employees, numbering upwards of six hundred within the building and one hundred and fifty without, together with a stable of forty or fifty horses constantly in active use. In extent, in completeness, in exact system, and in widespread business, few houses on the American continent compare with it. Besides shipments to every State and Territory of the American Union, the firm has constant transactions with England, Norway, Belgium, South America, Canada, Africa, China, Australia, and to all countries where importation of tobacco is not prohibited; and in all these countries they have regularly established agencies.

E. H. POGUE,

a manufacturer of plug tobacco at Hillsboro since 1873, transferred his business to Durham in April 1879, occupying a new building of wood, 40x100, with a deep brick basement, making a house of, practically, four stories high. At the beginning of his work in Durham, Mr. Pogue manufactured "plug" extensively, but has recently abandoned it, and in a measure substituted for it his "cut plug chewing tobacco," which is rapidly coming into use and favor. He also makes "twist" of superior excellence. But his specialties are his granulated "Sitting Bull" smoking tobacco, which has a wide sale and reputation, and his "Original and Genuine Durham Long Cut," branded according to grade No. 1 and 2; this is made out of the choicest stock and commands large sales, the principal demand being from St. Louis and Chicago, which are also made distributing points for contiguous territory. A large trade for this variety has also been established in New York, Philadelphia, and Baltimore.

The granulated "Sitting Bull" is known all over the United States, and upholds the reputation of Durham as a manufacturing point for smoking tobacco. The stock for this factory is all bought on the Durham market, and is exclusively the product of Orange and adjacent counties. The marked characteristics of the tobacco of this immediate section are exemplified in all the manufactures of Durham, and to a very large extent in those of other points, in Virginia especially, whose choicest supplies are drawn from this favored region.

The products of the year ending with May, 1880, were two hundred thousand pounds, since which time there has been a large increase of trade, especially in the " Long Cut," which has at once become a much-desired article of consumption ; but in all branches of his business Mr. Pogue exhibits a large and steady increase.

Very recently the manufacture of cigarettes has been introduced into this factory, claimed to be essentially different from and superior to anything now made.

W. DUKE, SONS & CO.

have grown from very modest beginnings to be among the largest and most successful manufacturers of Durham. The humble peddler of manufactured tobacco, ruined by the war, and compelled for subsistence to travel through the country selling from his wagon the small stock drawn by a pair of mules, all the ravages of war had left him, now presides over next to the largest business in the place.

Mr. W. Duke began the manufacture of smoking tobacco in the vicinity of Durham in the fall of the year 1865, removing to Durham during 1872 or 1873. Prospering by his transfer of locality, his business has expanded, requiring increase of room and facilities for manufacture. He, or rather the firm of W. Duke, Sons & Co., for he has associated with him three enterprising and experienced members of his family, now occupy a building of wood, three stories high, seventy feet long, with a frontage of eighty feet, with which is connected a house containing a steam engine which furnishes the power for grinding and cleaning the tobacco for market. The product is "granulated," the most widely known brand made being " The Duke of Durham." " Pro Bono Publico " is another fine brand, but " High Grab," unsurpassed in quality and selling readily at $1.00 per pound, is also largely made. The trade of this house extends throughout the United States, unconfined by section. Some shipments are made to London, and some to Cape Town, in Africa.

The stock is bought altogether on the Durham market. The annual product of the house is about seven hundred thousand pounds, but is so steadily and largely increasing that it promises far to exceed that point.

LUCIUS GREEN

began business in 1877, occupying a building of wood two and a half stories high and 70x30 in extent. Granulated tobacco of superior quality is the sole manufacture of this house. The standard brand is their " Indian Girl," but a more common brand, " O K," is also made, of both of which about fifty thousand pounds are annually made, with increasing business. The markets on which these brands are principally sold are New York, San Francisco, and Chicago, with growing reputation and increasing demand.

Isaac N. Link

succeeded W. R. Hughes & Co. in 1876 as a manufacturer of smoking tobacco, and has worked continuously under the above name since engaging in the business. He manufactures exclusively granulated tobacco, his sole brand being the " Dime Durham," of which his factory has a capacity of one thousand pounds a day, of a most superior fabric. This factory stands third in productiveness, as claimed by the proprietor, on the list of Durham factories. The work is continued through the year to meet a demand which is well sustained by the New York, Philadelphia, Cincinnati, and Chicago markets.

Z. J. Lyon & Co.

The firm comprising Z. J. and J. Ed. Lyon began the manufacture of tobacco in 1874, in a building of wood, two and a half stories high, and 32x70 feet. They use steam power, and employ sixteen hands on an average, making granulated exclusively, the annual product of which is about one hundred and seventy-eight thousand pounds. Their only brand is the "Pride of Durham," which finds markets in the Northern and New England States, with also some Southern and Western trade. In connection with this establishment is a box factory which supplies the trade of the place generally.

R. T. Faucett

began business in 1871, but was burned out in 1877, and rebuilt in another location the succeeding year. He now occupies a building of wood, two and a half stories high, and 80x40 feet in dimension. His product is granulated smoking tobacco, his brands being "Favorite Durham" and "Ten Cent Durham," with a trade extending all over the United States. The yearly product of the factory is about one hundred and eighty thousand pounds. Steam is used for grinding, cleaning, etc.

R. F. Morris & Son

were the real pioneers of tobacco manufacture in Durham, while J. R. Green was the originator of the brand that first gave it celebrity. R. F. Morris & Son began their manufacture in 1865, continuing it until the death of the senior partner, when a transfer was made, and the business is now conducted by W. H. Willard as president and S. F. Tomlinson as superintendent. The principal brand of this house is the " Bear," a granulated smoking tobacco of good repute which has an extensive general demand.

This house is also a large manufacturer of Scotch snuff, the only one of the kind in the State, and sustain their claim to make an article prepared with great care and skill, and free from adulterations prejudicial to health, and is made from pure clean stock, selected with careful reference to a good quality of snuff. A higher grade, Maccaboy, is also made, and both of them are in large demand.

ROULHAC & CO.

are manufacturers of the "Tiger" brand of granulated smoking tobacco. W. S. Roulhac began the business in Hillsboro in 1871, under the firm of Webb & Roulhac, but removed to Durham in 1873, with the same firm name, which was changed in 1876 to its present title. The house does a good business, principally with the North and Northwest, and its product is held in high repute.

J. R. DAY & BRO.

established their business in Nov. 1878, the firm having been composed of J. R. and W. P. Day. The former was one of the copartners of W. T. Blackwell & Co., and acquired large experience as a manufacturer, which at once gave the new association an impetus so great as to rival in amount of sales during the first year of their business the operations of any other house in Durham.

In January, 1880, the business was sold to H. K. and F. B. Thurber, of New York, who propose largely to increase the work of the house. The business is still carried on under the original name of the firm. Granulated tobacco is exclusively made, and the house has but one brand, that of "Standard of the World."

The business occupies their building of wood, two and a half stories high. Steam power is used for granulating and cleansing the tobacco.

CHAPTER IX.

HILLSBORO.

THIS point in Orange County, N. C., has been the seat of very consider-able manufacturing industry for more than twenty years. Situated very conveniently to the tobacco-producing regions of Orange, Person, Caswell, and Alamance counties, it occupied a position sufficiently commanding to have become a controlling power. There has been no development of enterprise commensurate with the advantages of situation. Yet the manufactures of Hillsboro have always been held in high repute; and it is believed now that the success of some already at work will have a beneficial effect upon others, who, until now, have held back through timidity or indolence.

Here the warehouse business, as in some other places, was not the creator of manufactures. It followed after the necessities for a supply at home became clamorous for satisfaction. Almost at once, in 1869–70, three warehouses came into existence. Two soon perished; but

Webb's Warehouse,

built in 1870, still survives, and with now good hope of permanent existence. It is a wooden building 125x40, and was originally conducted by J. C. Webb. He was succeeded by J. R. Gattis; he by E. H. Pogue; and Mr. C. B. Taylor is now proprietor. He opened the house on the 11th of March, 1880, and his sales to the 1st of October reached 250,000 pounds. In 1878, at which time E. H. Pogue was in charge, the sales reached 500,000 pounds. In 1879 the house was closed.

FACTORIES.

J. Y. Whitted began work in 1859 under the firm name of Webb & Whitted, and was at the head of a large and growing business at the opening of the war, when the house ceased operations. Business was resumed in 1867 by J. Y. Whitted under the firm name of J. Y. Whitted & Co., which firm has worked continuously ever since. Mr. Whitted occupies a building of wood, 110x40, two stories high, furnished with the most approved machinery. The product is plug and twist; and recently a fine brand of smoking tobacco, "Harry Lee," which is becoming widely and popularly known. The choicest brands of plug are "Gold Ambrosia," which has taken the first premiums and medals at four of the North Carolina State Fairs, the first premium at the Alabama State Fair, and the same at the Atlanta, Savannah and Wilmington Agricultural Fairs. It was exhibited at Vienna, but arrived after the awards had been made.

Next in order is "Harry Lee," "North State," "Walter Raleigh" and "J. Y. Whitted's Sun Cured." The markets for these brands are in North and South Carolina, Georgia, Alabama, Texas, Florida and Louisiana, also Tennessee and Virginia. The annual product is now one hundred thousand pounds, with increasing business.

WEBB & CO.

is the firm name conducting the factory known as Webb's, the firm being composed of James Webb, Jr., J. C. Webb and Geo. C. Corbin. They began work in 1878 in a wooden building, but in 1880 erected a brick edifice, four stories high and 40x60, using this in connection with the old premises. The product is twist and plug, the latter largely in excess of the former. Their best brands are "Superb," "Choice Bright," "Choice Red." Their stocks are bought on all markets. The product this year is about one hundred and fifty thousand pounds, with a large prospective increase. Their markets are mostly in North Carolina and the Southern States generally. Their twist is sent mostly to Cincinnati and Nashville. The brands are "Berkshire" and "Victory."

H. P. JONES & CO.

organized their business in 1872. They occupy a wooden building two stories high, 150x50. Their operations are conducted by steam power. This is exclusively "a smoking" factory. The only brands made are "Occonneechee" and "Tar Heel," both granulated, and a superior article of "long cut," also branded "Tar Heel." The product is about fifty thousand pounds, with decided indications of very large future increase.

These tobaccos are very popular wherever known, and are growing steadily in favor. At present, the markets are New York, Georgia and the Western States. Occasional shipments are made to Liverpool, Berlin and the Coast of Africa. A large trade has been opened with Cincinnati for "Occonneechee," and active agencies established in the city of New York, besides important business with Chicago. All the stock used by this house is bought on the Hillsboro market.

GRAHAM & CO.

succeed to the business initiated by J. W. Corbin in 1871, who worked until 1873, when the factory was worked under the name of Corbin & Pogue for one year, and then again for one year by J. W. Corbin. He suspended for one year, and operations were resumed by J. M. Corbin, who was succeeded during 1880 by the present firm. This occupies a wooden building two stories high, 30x60. The product is plug and twist of all styles. The best brands are "No. 1," "No. 2," "No. 3" and "No. 4," and "J. W. Corbin." plug, and "Little Carrie," twist. The shipments are principally to Nashville, Memphis, Cincinnati, Chicago, St. Joseph, and to

Arkansas. The product for this year, 1880, is about one hundred thousand pounds, and increases steadily, next year's business being expected to be much larger.

REIDSVILLE,

in Rockingham County, is situated on the line of the Richmond and Danville Railroad, equidistant from Greensboro in North Carolina and Danville in Virginia, twenty-five miles from each. It is, like Durham, the creation of the tobacco interest. Rockingham County had long been devoted largely to the cultivation of tobacco, which was cultivated mostly on the rich and heavy lands along Dan river and its tributaries, the product being either the dark rich mahogany suitable for wrappers and fillers or the coarser shipping tobacco, all of which found sale in the markets of Virginia. But the newly designated station was also convenient to the county of Caswell, more famous than Rockingham because of the finer quality of its tobacco, and not far remote from the counties of Person and Alamance in North Carolina, and from some of the best producing counties in Virginia, and manufactories and warehouses were established and rapidly increased in number, until Reidsville is now an important point both of receipt and manufacture. Of the former, the warehouse sales for the season ending October 1st, 1880, reached about four million pounds, and there were manufactured for the same period about two million pounds. There are three warehouses in Reidsville.

REDD'S WAREHOUSE

was opened on the 19th of April, 1875, by J. S. Redd and J. F. Wooten. The present proprietors are J. S. Redd, J. F. Wooten, J. Willie Smith and J. A. Roach. The building is of wood on a brick basement, and is 50x125 feet, well lighted, conveniently arranged, with extensive adjoining lots for stabling, etc. The sales are held daily. The supplies of tobacco are drawn from the surrounding counties of both Virginia and North Carolina. There is a steady annual increase in the business of this house, which is somewhat more than a third of that of the Reidsville market.

THE PIEDMONT WAREHOUSE,

the proprietor of which is A. J. Ellington, was established in 1871, and is a brick building 50x120, of excellent arrangement within and without. The sales are daily; the receipts, like those of Redd's, are from the surrounding counties. A large amount of shipped tobacco is also sold here.

There is also another warehouse, the Eagle, from which no information was obtained.

There are a number of factories in operation, and several at present closed. Among the former is the smoking factory of

DENNY, SMITH & CO.,

who began business in 1880, working during that year on a scale somewhat smaller than will mark their operations hereafter. They manufacture a granulated smoking tobacco, their only brand being the "Monogram," which has gained high favor in the markets into which it has been introduced. It is sold principally in the South and also in St. Louis. The business of this house shows such steady and healthy increase as to justify the purpose largely to increase the size of the buildings during the coming winter.

HARRISS, SAMPSON & CO.

began business under the above style in 1879, occupying two buildings in different parts of the town, the one of wood and brick, three stories high, 40x90 feet, and supplied with the most perfect machinery. In this an average of one hundred and twenty-five hands are employed, who made during the past season three hundred and fifty thousand pounds of plug and twist. The other building is fifty feet square, three stories high, and employs from eighty to ninety hands, who will make during the season ending with November 1st, 1880, one hundred and seventy-five thousand pounds twist. The supplies of material are obtained on the Reidsville market.

R. A. ELLINGTON & SONS

were engaged in manufacturing in Wentworth, in Rockingham County, North Carolina, for several years, and transferred their business to Reidsville in 1880, occupying a wooden building with stone basement, 40x80 feet, and three stories high. About sixty hands are employed, who make annually one hundred thousand pounds of plug and twist, which is shipped largely to Eastern Carolina and to Georgia and Alabama. The proprietors say their business increases steadily.

MOTLEY, WRIGHT & CO.

began business in 1879. They occupy a brick building four stories high and 133x44 feet. Their machinery is of the most approved construction and their hydraulic presses are acted on by steam power. They employ about two hundred hands and produce five hundred thousand pounds of plug and twist. Next year they propose to manufacture eight hundred thousand pounds. Their trade is with Georgia, Alabama, Mississippi, Louisiana and Texas.

D. BARNES & CO.

entered into their present business in 1872-3 as Barnes & Crofts. The present firm is composed of D. Barnes, John D. Staples and P. H. Williamson, organized in 1879. They occupy a building of wood, two and a half stories high, 80x40. They use the most perfect machinery and produce plug exclusively, of which they make during the current year one hundred and fifty thousand pounds, finding ready markets in Georgia, Alabama and Mississippi principally.

F. R. PENN & Co.

The firm, being composed of F. R. & S. C. Penn, engaged in their present business in 1874, occupying now a building partly of wood, partly of brick, four stories high and 40x126 feet. They employ one hundred and twenty-five hands, who will produce during the present working season three hundred and seventy-five thousand pounds of plug and twist, which is sold mostly in the Southern States. Their business steadily develops, their first year's product being seventy-five thousand pounds. They doubled the capacity of their building last winter, and propose during the coming winter to apply steam in their operations.

WATT & HIGHTOWER

organized as a firm in May, 1880, manufacturing plug and twist to the extent of about one hundred and twenty-five thousand pounds yearly. They work principally for jobbers for Atlanta, Montgomery, Savannah, Macon and Mobile, making both twist and plug. They report their business increasing beyond expectation, with bright future prospects.

Several other houses in Reidsville, now closed, will resume work in the working season of 1881.

In the county of Rockingham, in which Reidsville is situated, there are other factories at Leaksville, Madison and Wentworth, some of which are closed during this year. The whole amount of revenue collected on tobacco for this county in the year 1879 was $244,930.67.

OXFORD.

This beautiful town is in the centre of a fine agricultural country, where the production of the cereals, of cotton and of tobacco, is combined in equal excellence in a rare contiguity. Around the town and along the roads leading to it may be found farms upon which all these staples are embraced in one glance of the eye, and the appearance of all indicative of soil and climate happily adapted to the utmost perfection of each and all of them. Tobacco in this county attains its very highest excellence. The experienced dealer in tobacco can tell at a glance or detect by the touch the celebrated Dutchville leaf—a bright yellow that has never found an equal. Other sections of the county are scarcely inferior, and the quality of the land and the nice experience of the planters have given, for a number of years, a distinguished prominence to Granville.

But until recently she has found her markets abroad. Her planters have gone to Petersburg, to Richmond, to Danville, and, of later years, to

Durham—these two latter of late years being the generally preferred points, though Richmond retains a firm hold upon the preferences of many.

In 1878 Mr. H. G. Cooper, of Oxford, sagaciously saw the opportunity to found a business which would retain a portion of the trade at home, and erected a warehouse, which speedily proved the wisdom of the movement. During the first year the sales reached three hundred thousand pounds.

Messrs. Kingsbury, Minor & Lassiter and Mr. E. H. Crew opened warehouses in 1880, and during that year the aggregate sales were two million pounds of farmer's tobacco, which is bought on order or on speculation.

There is a small manufacturing industry here—three plug factories in operation.

HENDERSON,

situated on the Raleigh and Gaston Railroad, in the county of Granville, within a few years has acquired prominence as a tobacco market. In the centre of a fertile agricultural region, it had grown steadily, from its foundation in 1838, to considerable importance as the market, or at least shipping point, for the cotton and the cereals raised in the adjacent counties; and in turn the distributing centre for the merchandise, the fertilizers and other supplies needed for the agricultural classes; and was also the shipping and receiving point for Oxford, the flourishing county-seat of Granville. Nearly destroyed by fire in 1870, it had been rebuilt, and was ready for the impetus given to its growth by the addition of the tobacco business.

In addition to Granville, the adjacent counties of Warren and Franklin soon found Henderson their most convenient market; and the enterprise of warehousemen and manufacturers was evoked to supply such convenience. Warehouses and factories both now meet every demand, and Henderson is now one of the large tobacco markets in the State.

WAREHOUSES.

There are three of these.

The proprietors of the " Cooper's Warehouse " erected their building in 1873—a structure of wood, 150x150, with all needed conveniences. This house controls a very large business and claims to have the largest wagon trade in the State.

CURRIN & WATKINS,

of " Watkins Warehouse," built in 1877 their warehouse, of wood, 40x182, and they also do a large business.

J. S. MEADOWS,

of the Meadows Warehouse, built in 1873. They have a house of wood, 40x120.

All of these houses are well lighted and well arranged both for buyer and seller.

The supplies for these houses come from the counties of Granville, Warren and Franklin in North Carolina and Mecklenburg in Virginia. The supply is altogether farmer's tobacco. There is little or no shipped tobacco on the market; and this, together with a uniformly high grade, leads to the claim of the Henderson market that the averages here are higher than on any other market.

The sales of the year ending October 1st, 1879, were six million pounds. It is thought that the sales to October 1st, 1880, reached ten millions. They are stated elsewhere in these pages at seven millions.

FACTORIES.

Jos. E. Pogue

manufactures plug exclusively. His tobacco has gained large reputation. At the State Fair in 1879 he took the first premium for quality, and at the Fair of 1880 the premium for the best and largest exhibit of manufactured tobacco. Markets mostly in North Carolina.

W. E. Gary & Co.

make both plug and smoking, with a trade confined principally to the Southern States.

Perry & Bros.

began the manufacture of smoking tobacco in 1880, their brand being "Clear the Track."

PRIZE HOUSES.

Of these there are several, occupied by leaf dealers who buy and ship on their own account. S. & C. Watkins occupy a building of wood, 40x98, with five floors; C. Hunter, a building 40x80; J. D. Cooper, one 30x100; J. H. Lassiter one 30x60, and R. M. Powell one of the same size.

ROXBORO,

in Person County, is the centre of large tobacco culture. The planters have always stood high for skill in culture. From absence of railroad facilities, manufacture became almost a necessity, and, at Roxboro, Woodsdale, Blue Wing, and other points in the county, before the war many factories existed. Under changed conditions, Roxboro alone continues to manufacture. A warehouse was indispensable, and therefore Messrs. Webb & Co. opened one in 1875. It is a commodious wooden building, 40x80 feet, with skylight and every accommodation for the farmer. The tobacco sold here is almost all of home production. The sales for the year will reach three hundred thousand pounds.

FACTORIES.

J. P. Satterfield began the enterprise of the cigar manufacture in 1878. He uses Pennsylvania and Connecticut leaf. His brands have achieved a high reputation: " Little Mamie," " Odd Fellow," and " Pride of America." He also manufactures the "South Down" smoking tobacco.

LONG'S.

W. H. Long established his factory in 1874, for plug and twist. His building is of wood, 30x124, two and a half stories high. The product of the factory is one hundred thousand pounds annually. He works sixty hands, using hydraulic machinery.

W. C. SATTERFIELD

manufactures plug and fancy twist, making sixty thousand pounds per annum. His building is of wood, 40x70, two and a half stories high. He works forty-five hands, using hydraulic power.

DANVILLE,

in Pittsylvania County, Virginia, is so intimately associated with the tobacco interests of North Carolina that it must unavoidably be named in the same connection, for it was the exclusive market for many years for the border counties of the latter State, affording facilities not to be had at home, and, from its proximity to the border, the large influx of North Carolina merchants, manufacturers, and residents, becoming to all intents and purposes a North Carolina town, identical in habits, interests, and pursuits. Its growth is largely due to the tobacco business, which is now, as it always has been, the paramount interest, stimulated and developed by the construction of the railroad to Richmond, about the year 1847, still further stimulated by the connection with the North Carolina railroad system during the existence of the war, awaiting still wider development by the narrow-gauge roads now under construction to Henry County, and anticipating still greater advantages from the building of the Midland Road into regions not yet penetrated by her enterprise. With every advantage of water power, Danville has confined the use of its capital and enterprise almost exclusively to the sale and manufacture of tobacco—potent elements' of prosperity, however, which prove their influence by the growth of a town in a few years from a court-house seat of small population to a city of ten thousand inhabitants, well built, well paved, lighted with gas, supplied with abundant water, and having eight sales-warehouses and nearly thirty tobacco factories, all of them large and commodious brick buildings, and producing annually about fifteen million pounds of manufactured tobacco.

The warehouse system was established before the war by Mr. Neal, for the convenience both of the manufacturer and the farmer, the former having previously to go into the country and purchase his stock at the barns, and the latter, if he brought his crop to market, making his sales in the streets, with all the inconvenience of exposure to weather and unfavorable presentation of the qualities of his products. No development, however, of the warehouse system was made until the superior advantages of bringing buyer and seller face to face, and under the stimulus of competition, was demonstrated, hastened also by some of the requirements of the newly-enacted revenue laws, which enforced greater exactness in the transfer of an article become so important a subject of taxation. Sales otherwise are now , not usually made, though buyers frequently make their contracts with the farmers at the barns, a mode which is only justified by the sagacious experience of the purchaser and the perfect integrity and good faith of the seller.

The increase in the sales in the warehouses has been steadily progressive, as is shown by the exhibits of a few years. In 1873-4, they were about 12,000,000 pounds; in 1874-5, 14,679,421, of the average value of $20.45 per hundred pounds: in 1875-6, 23,466,413, averaging $13.32; in 1876-7, 16,426,296, with an average of $12.38; in 1877-8, 27,698,828; in 1878-9, 26,827,924; and in 1879-80, 33,151,310.

To handle this large amount, eight warehouses are now engaged, and the stability of the business is evinced by the elegant and substantial buildings devoted to the purpose, in strong contrast to the structures originally used, one or two of which still survive as mementos of the infancy of a now fully developed institution.

GRAVES' WAREHOUSE

exists as one of the oldest in construction in Danville. Capt. W. P. Graves, the proprietor, is from Caswell County, a veteran of the Mexican war, and began the sales business in Neal's, the first warehouse opened in Danville, in 1858, where he remained until he went into the service of the Southern Confederacy as commander of the Danville Blues in 1861. In April, 1867, he built the original building of Holland's warehouse, which he occupied one year. In 1868 he erected his present warehouse, where he has ever since remained. This building is 175x80, of wood, and is conveniently arranged. W. P. Graves is proprietor; George E. Coleman, auctioneer; Joseph H. Blackwell, floor manager; F. L. Walker, clerk; Col. O. L. Bailey and P. H. Tredway, assistant clerks. The supplies, as with all other warehouses in Danville, are from the adjacent counties of Virginia and North Carolina, and with receipts from very distant points in those States, the mountain counties in both of late making many shipments to Danville. Of these receipts, brights predominate. The sales in this house fluctuate. In 1872-73 they were 2,986,449 pounds, with an average of $12.13 per cent.; in 1873-74 they were 2,136,249, average $10; in 1874-75, 4,112,748, average $18.94; in 1875-76, 4,084,811, average $10.10; in 1876-77, 2,601,426, average $10.60; in 1877-78, 2,596,-235, and in 1879-80 about 3,000,000.

HOLLAND'S WAREHOUSE

was established in 1867. Originally of wood, it has given place to a commodious and admirably arranged structure of brick which was erected in 1878, and which is 100x208, with ample storage rooms in the basement. The salesroom is well lighted with solid skylights. The proprietors are S. H. Holland, Daniel Coleman and Peter B. Law, who constitute the oldest warehouse firm in Danville. The officers are J. W. Guerrant, of Rockingham County, N. C., floor manager; Daniel Coleman and J. J. Hill, auctioneers, and P. B. Law, book-keeper. The annual sales are over five million pounds. The sales were made up, for the past year, mostly of brights, peculiar to this section, and a small proportion of fine and fancy wrappers, or what are called first-class fillers. Between Virginia and North Carolina there is little difference in supplies, with possibly an excess in favor of the former.

THE STAR WAREHOUSE

was established in 1874 by Pace Bros., now of Lynchburg, who had previously occupied a large but roughly constructed wooden building. In that year they erected the large brick building now occupied by Hutchings, Thomas & Co., the first of those substantial and conveniently arranged warehouses so marked a feature of Danville. This building is 150x160, with an area of twenty-four thousand square feet of floor surface, with a large basement for the storage of tobacco. The sales of this house are now largely in excess of five million pounds yearly, as by following table:
Sold by Hutchings, Thomas & Co., from 1st October, 1872, to   .

DATE.		POUNDS.	PRICE.	TOTAL.
1st Oct.,	1873	2,122,873	$11.36	$241,266.13
"	1874	2,829,988	15.62	441,985.94
"	1875	2,329,199	20.83	485,225.47
"	1876	3,812,883	14.24	543,109.41
"	1877	3,489,384	14.70	512,681.49
"	1878	5,260,729	14.60	768,382.02
"	1879	5,252,925	11.22	589,488.27

THE FARMER'S WAREHOUSE,

by Redd & Jordan, is a large and commodious brick building, erected on the site of the wooden structure burned the preceding year. The present building is 190x80, with an L 40x50, with excellent arrangements for planters and teams. The receipts of this house, embracing everything but shipping tobacco, are from Henry, Halifax and Pittsylvania counties in Virginia and from the border counties of North Carolina. Brights predominate. The sales of the crop of 1879–80 are estimated at four million pounds.

The Cabell Warehouse

was erected in November, 1877, and is a wooden building 190x110, with a lot extending from Bridge to Craghead and Main streets, with extensive accommodations for teams, one hundred and fifty stalls, a camp-house of brick, two stories high, and a three-story storage house for tobacco held for sale. The heaviest receipts are from Halifax County, in Virginia, and the border counties of North Carolina, chiefly Caswell and Rockingham. Brights predominate, but the receipts of mahogany wrappers and fillers from Henry and Rockingham are large. The receipts from the crop of 1879-80 are estimated at five millions.

The Public Warehouse,

by Thomas L. Poindexter & Son, was erected in 1877 and is of wood, 170x70, with a wing 40x60. Receipts of all grades are from the neighboring counties of Virginia and North Carolina. Large sales are made on orders, and the sales this year will exceed five million pounds.

The Banner Warehouse

was opened on the 19th of November, 1879, the proprietors being J. B. Anderson & Co. The building is of brick, 160x80, and is admirably lighted and is altogether one of the most perfect structures of its kind in use. A new feature in it is that baggage and harness are checked as in hotels.

Mr. C. C. Anderson is auctioneer; N. L. Johnson, of Caswell County, North Carolina, and J. H. Cole, of Halifax, Virginia, are floor managers.

The sales for this year are about three and one-half million pounds, with an average of twelve and three-quarter cents.

Neal's Warehouse.

No information furnished.

The Annual Report of the President of the Tobacco Association of Danville (Mr. Ferrall), made for the year closing September 30, 1880, shows that the receipts of leaf for the year amounted to 33,151,310 pounds, selling on the warehouse floors for $3,775,500.79, or an average of $11.38 per hundred.

Of this it is estimated that North Carolina furnished nearly, if not quite, one-half—the location of Danville being such that it commands the North Carolina trade as much as she does that of Virginia.

Danville is a very important manufacturing point, there being about thirty factories of the largest and most substantial character used for the manufacture of plug tobacco; but these are only referred to, not being essential to the objects of this publication.

CHAPTER X.

BURDENS ON TOBACCO.

GOVERNMENTS may fairly be permitted, in provision for their main-tenance, to select such objects for the imposition of the burden of taxation, from which essential revenue is derived, as may justly fall under the head of luxuries. The common sense of mankind assigns to superfluities responsibilities from which necessaries of life should be freed. But in the changed subjects of modern tastes and habits, it is difficult to draw the distinction between what are luxuries and what are necessaries. What was once accessible only to the rich and grateful only to the refined, the larger intercourse of nations has brought within the reach of all. High prices may no longer erect a barrier between the rich and the poor; and the favored taste of a special class has become the common relish of the masses. And there would be no restriction upon the common enjoyment of so-called luxuries did not Government step in, and, by the imposition of duties or taxes, revive a distinction which time had almost effaced. In nothing has this distinction been more arbitrarily asserted and enforced than in the article of tobacco, scarcely to be called a luxury, since it has become so indispensable to the comfort of the human race. And in nothing is this distinction so unjust, because it is enforced upon a solitary subject of agricultural toil. Foreign governments may be pardoned for their exactions upon articles of distant growth. A home government shows deficiency in parental interest, rather displays the animosity of a foster parent, when it singles out tobacco alone of all agricultural produce as the mark for heavy discrimination and vindictive oppression. The results of the war made the South sensible that it had many of its after burdens to bear, but the terms of settlement could not lead her to expect so unequal an apportionment of them. They were imposed, however, when the Southern States had no voice in acts of national legislation, when the voice of the victor clamorously dictated the policy of the Government, and when prostrate provinces offered a rich and ready spoil in the wealth of special objects of universal consumption. The civilized world, the North itself, called a halt when the heavy hand of taxation was laid on cotton, because that staple had interwoven itself into the interests and sympathies of every industrial community. But tobacco, the special subject of Southern culture and manufacture, has found no friends with any administration, and though the tax has fluctuated from forty cents down to sixteen cents upon the pound, it endures even at this lowest rate a burden on the most abundant grades, of from one to four hundred per cent. No such burden has ever oppressed an Anglo-Saxon agricultural class; and it is one amazing to the newly created African citizens, large producers of tobacco, who, in all other particulars, have been the signal recipients of governmental favors.

In the imposition of the tax on tobacco, certain axioms have been disregarded. " In a free government taxes are laid by the representatives of the people, and of course with the consent of those who are to pay them." If ours is now a free government, which it certainly was not in respect to an important section at the time the revenue laws were enacted, it is theoretically proper and justly right that that revenue be now revised to approximate equality in burdens. It can never be just, however it may be temporarily productive, to oppress one special industry. Again : " every tax ought to be so apportioned as to take out, and keep out, of the pockets of the people as little as possible over and above of what it brings into the public treasury of the State." The revenue law of the United States disregards this absolutely. It takes out, and it puts nothing back. It robs the producer, and affects all others. To use the language of the Hon. Geo. C. Cabell, M. C. from Virginia :

✓ " The producer suffers because his, of all other agricultural products, is singled out for taxation ; that his industrial pursuit, to which he is compelled by the peculiarities of climate, soil and habit, is heavily burdened, his bone and muscle, his energy, his toil, his poverty, are all made to pay tribute to the Government, while other sections, other industries, and other productions go free of tax, and, indeed, are made to prosper by reason of the very impositions upon tobacco.

" The manufacturer suffers because he must carry, at vast outlay, not only his stock but his stamps ; because he is hedged about by annoying regulations, and is subjected not only to the ordinary vicissitudes of trade, but to the constant agitation which ever attends an onerous tax.

" The consumer suffers because, having contracted the free use of tobacco, he regards it more as a necessity than a luxury ; because many of the poorer classes, the greatest consumers, by the enhanced price consequent upon the tax are driven in great degree from the market, and forced to the use of the meaner grades of tobacco, while the rich alone can indulge in the luxury of the fine.

" The Government suffers because the tax rate is so high that it discourages production, manufacture, and consumption, promotes fraud, paralyzes trade, and, in short, by its oppressiveness defeats in great degree the ends and objects of the whole revenue system."

The product of North Carolina for the year 1880 is not less than forty-six million of pounds. The average value of this is about twelve cents, or $5,552,000. The tax is sixteen cents a pound, or $7,360,000.

The tax is the more onerous because the imposition of an authority which will not be convinced of unwisdom or injustice, and because, in many parts of the South, it is the only money crop, the only profitable crop adapted to many soils—a crop made and perfected by hereditary habit and skill, and one, therefore, not readily abandoned.

But if the production of tobacco is oppressed at home, how much more kindly or wisely is it welcomed abroad ? Great Britain closes all but thirteen of her many ports against it, and in these thirteen graciously permits its reception upon the payment of a duty of 3s. per pound without regard to quality, and if it contains less than 10 per cent. of moisture 3s. 6d.—the shilling being about 23 cents. France, Austria, Spain and Italy all control a monopoly of tobacco through the agency of the Regie system. These governments enter into contracts with certain of their subjects who engage to furnish a certain quantity at a stipulated price. These contractors naturally pay as little as they can to make as much as they can out of their contract. The amount contracted for is restricted, therefore over-production, or even the normal crop of the United States, finds no Continental market open to the caprices or changes of demand. The quality purchased is inferior, therefore the producer has no encouragement for the increased culture of superior grades. The contractor may lose by his contract; but his government, using its power of monopoly with relentless force, adds largely to its revenues.

To illustrate the operations of the Regie system in France the following, from the New York *Commercial Bulletin* of July, 1880, is quoted, premising that the reports of the Regie for 1874 had only recently been published and the statistics of that year only are available.

The quantity of tobacco purchased by the French government in 1875 and 1874 respectively was as follows:

	1875.	1874.
Domestic and foreign tobacco	17,900,863	16,748,599
Cigars and cigarettes	12,864,388	21,663,686
Total, kilos	30,666,251	38,412,285

The average price of the home crop of France in 1875 was 90f. 66c. per 100 kilos, and Algerian brought 62f. 79c. In 1874 the averages were respectively 89f. 89c. and 75f. 34c. The production of tobacco in France was in 1874 13,828,486 kilos and in Algeria 4,850,043 kilos. The purchases in 1874 and in 1875, with the average price paid per 100 kilos (in francs), were as follows:

The kilo or kilogramme is 2½ pounds and the franc is 18¾ cents.

American	1875 Kilos.	1875 Price.	1874 Kilos.	1874 Price.
Virginia	1,127,155	133.77	1,849,882	112.22
Kentucky	630,778	134.33	5,637,548	114.63
Maryland	2,239,213	128.41	5,988,023	112.10
Brazil	509,068	232.99	215,414	217.86
New Grenada	121	204.49	....	....
Mexico	1,037	300.00	....	....
San Domingo	91	301.64	275	235.89
Seed Leaf	173,990	122.07	1,927	167.53
Rio Grande	297,727	193.82	544	202.87
Havana	115,515	663.03	60,418	815.93
Total	5,004,696	....	13,754,084	....

The average price was 1,007.99f. per 100 kilos. The profits of the French government monopoly ranged from 177,920,000f. in 1865 to 254,557,000f. in 1875, which is one of the easiest ways of making revenue for a government we know of.

The franc is nearly one-fifth of a dollar, so that the government, in these two years, made respectively a profit of $35,580,000 and $50,911,400.

In other foreign countries the duties are as follows :

In Germany the duty on leaf tobacco and stems is 85 marks per 100 kilogrammes, equal to 10.40 cents per pound; on strips and scraps, 180 marks per 100 kilogrammes, equal to 22.05 cents per pound; on manufactured tobacco and cigars, 170 marks per 100 kilogrammes, equal to 33.08 cents per pound. On tobacco produced in Germany, the tax taking effect after April 1, 1880: From April 1, 1880, to March 31, 1881, 10 marks per 180 kilogrammes, equal to 2.45 cents per pound; from April 1, 1881, to March 31, 1882, 30 marks per 100 kilogrammes, equal to 3.67 cents per pound; from April 1, 1882, and thereafter 45 marks per 100 kilogrammes, equal to 5.50 cents per pound. In Belgium the impost is reckoned after deducting 15 per cent. for tare. The duty is 20f. ($3.86 gold) per 100 kilogrammes (100 American pounds equal to 45½ kilogrammes). In Holland the duty is 28 cents gold per 100 kilogrammes (280 American pounds being equal to 127 kilogrammes). In Russia the duty on leaf tobacco is 4 roubles 10 kopecks per pud; on smoking tobacco 26 roubles 40 kopecks per pud (the pud is about 36 American pounds). In Turkey the duty is 50 cents gold per 11½ American ounces. In England the duties are, on unmanufactured: Stemmed or stripped and unstemmed, containing 10 pounds or more of moisture in every 100 pounds weight thereof, 3s. 6d. per pound; containing less than 10 pounds of moisture, 3s. 10d. per pound. On manufactured tobacco: Cavendish and Negrohead, 4s. 10d. per pound; all other sorts, including cigarettes, 4s. 6d. per pound. In addition to the above duties there is a charge of ½ per cent. warehouse charges on all descriptions.— *Western Tobacco Journal.*

CANADIAN TOBACCO DUTIES AND EXCISE.

The following are the rates of duty now imposed in Canada on the various manufactures of tobacco: Cigars and cigarettes, 50 cents per pound and 20 per cent. ad valorem. Manufactured tobacco, 25 cents per pound and 12½ per cent. ad valorem. Snuff, 25 cents per pound and 12½ per cent. ad valorem. In lieu of all excise duties—except license fees—now imposed on tobacco known as "common Canadian twist," otherwise called "tabac blanc en torquette," being the unpressed leaf rolled and twisted, and made wholly from raw tobacco, the growth of Canada, and upon raw leaf, the growth of Canada, there shall be imposed, levied and collected on every pound or less quantity than a pound an excise duty of four cents.

Our own government is not behind others in its readiness to impose its burden upon tobacco. The following are the taxes laid, which produced to the government, in 1879, a revenue on 170,722,000 pounds consumed at home, and including tax on cigars, cigarettes, snuff, special tax on manufacturers, dealers, etc., $41,115,528.

The tax on all kinds of manufactured tobacco is 16 cents per pound; snuff, 16 cents per pound; cigars, $6 per thousand; cigarettes weighing not over three pounds per thousand, $1.75 per thousand; cigarettes and cheroots weighing over three pounds per thousand, $6 per thousand. The duty on foreign cigars is $2.50 per pound and 25 per cent. ad valorem. Cigarettes same duty as cigars. Imported cigars, cigarettes and cheroots also bear the prescribed internal revenue taxes, to be paid by stamps at the custom house. The import duty on leaf tobacco is 35 cents per pound; leaf tobacco, stemmed, 50 cents per pound; manufactured tobacco, 50 cents per pound; scraps, 50 cents per pound. Manufactured tobacco and scraps are also subject to the internal revenue tax of 16 cents per pound, and must be packed in conformity with internal revenue laws and regulations. Scraps and cuttings, however, may be withdrawn in bulk for use in a tobacco, snuff or cigar manufactory without payment of the internal revenue tax.— *Western Tobacco Journal.*

Retail dealers in leaf tobacco are required to pay a special tax of $500, and if their annual sales amount to over $1,000 they must pay an additional tax of fifty cents for every dollar in excess of $1,000 of their sales. The tax upon dealers in leaf tobacco, those who buy and sell on commission original and unbroken hogsheads, bales and cases, is $25.00; but merchants may buy from planters, upon the payment of a license tax of $5, to an extent not exceeding 25,000 pounds per annum.

Farmers and planters are not required to pay any tax on tobacco of their own raising, or that received by them as rent from tenants who have produced the same on their land. Neither will the farmer be required to pack or prize his tobacco before offering it for sale, in hogsheads or otherwise, but he may sell it loose as he has heretofore been in the habit of selling, irrespective of taxation. If, however, he sells direct to consumers, or if he sells, assigns, consigns, transfers or disposes of his tobacco to persons other than those who have paid special taxes, either as leaf dealers or as manufacturers of tobacco, snuff or cigars, or to persons purchasing leaf for export, he becomes liable, as a retail dealer in leaf tobacco, to the special tax of $500, and to the additional tax of fifty cents on every dollar in excess of $1000 of his sales. It is the duty of every farmer producing and selling leaf tobacco, on demand of any revenue officer, to furnish a complete statement, verified by oath, of the amount of his sales, to whom sold, and where shipped.

In brief, the revenue laws provide:

No tax on the raw material.

Wholesale license, $25.00.

Retail license, $5.00, and 50 cents on each one dollar in excess of sales over $1000.

Snuff, 16 cents per pound.

Chewing and smoking tobaccos, 16 cents per pound.

The producer is at the mercy of systems which combine against him at home and abroad. At home, in the presence of a great national debt, diminishing by slow degrees, and in pursuance of a policy which practically operates upon the South as upon conquered territory, there is small hope of relief. Abroad, the same necessity is laid upon Great Britain and upon most of the continental powers. The abolition of the Regie system may be effected by interested negotiation. Should that be done, then a wide market would be thrown open to such grades of American tobacco as would bear the imposition of high duties. For it may be assumed that such measures would be followed by imposts somewhat akin to those of Great Britain. Fine qualities alone could bear those imposts. It would, therefore, be the policy of the North Carolina planter to direct his attention mainly to the production of such. The enlarging field for the production of " bright yellow tobacco " must have larger opening for continued profitable demand. That may follow when the Regie system gives place to something conformable to modern ideas of commerce.

CHAPTER XI.

TOTAL CROP OF NORTH CAROLINA.

IT is evident that no accurate account of the crop of North Carolina has ever been given. The U. S. statistician, in his report to the Department of Agriculture for the year 1878, the last that has been made public, excuses his inaccuracies by the difficulty of finding persons who are capable and willing to furnish reliable estimates, and remarks, that "the National census never agrees with State returns." There have never been accurate returns from this State, either National or State. But the returns from the Department at Washington are accepted abroad as authentic. The effect, of course, is to diminish North Carolina as a tobacco-producing State, and to confirm the secondary position she has been made to assume.

The report for 1878 assigns to North Carolina even a lower place than it occupied in 1860. In the former year, it is credited with only 12,896,000 pounds on an acreage of 20,800, with a total valuation of crop of $773,760.

Surely there have been no steps backward, and though tobacco has been so heavily oppressed by the exactions of onerous taxation, the soils and climates of certain sections, the habits of the planters, and the necessities of the people, have compelled an adherence to the culture of this staple. And the opening of markets at home, and the expansion of the warehouse system, have stimulated production so largely that even in 1878 the report of the statistician was enormously inaccurate.

It is not possible to give exact information, even from the source most to be relied on for accuracy—the warehouses, both in North Carolina and Virginia, in which the crop of the former is sold—because, in addition to what is technically called "farmer's tobacco," that is, tobacco delivered on the floors of the warehouses by the planters in person, there is always a large amount of "package tobacco"—that is, tobacco bought on one market and transhipped for sale to another market—sold in every warehouse, which goes to make up the aggregate amount of sales.

Making due allowance for this, the crop of 1880 may be safely estimated as follows, the conclusions having been reached by actual and personal inquiry :

The markets in North Carolina are : Durham, Winston, Reidsville, Henderson, Oxford, Milton, Hickory, Asheville, Hillsboro, and Marshall. The sales of farmer's tobacco were as follows: Durham, 8,000,000 pounds ; Winston, 7,000,000 ; Reidsville, 4,500,000 ; Henderson, 6,500,000 ; Oxford, 2,000,000 ; Milton, 2,000,000 ; Hickory, 250,000 ; Hillsboro, 250,000, and Marshall, 200,000—total 30,500,000.

The sales at Danville for the season of 1880 were, in round numbers,

34,000,000 pounds, of which one-half, at least, is to be credited to North Carolina. The sales of North Carolina tobacco in Richmond far exceed 20,000,000 of pounds, two million of which, at least, is farmer's tobacco;· Lynchburg sells at least one million pounds of North Carolina farmer's tobacco; South Boston as much, and Petersburg about the same—a total of 22,000,000 pounds sold in Virginia, which, added to the 30,500,000 sold in the North Carolina markets, gives a total of 52,500,000 pounds.

Even if over-estimated, which is not believed to be the case, the facts are sufficient to justify the demand that North Carolina shall have its recognition by foreign markets as a tobacco centre equally with Virginia, Kentucky, Maryland and Missouri, and should be entitled to a distinct classification for her distinctive qualities. She is almost the sole producer —a small portion of Virginia being the only exception—of the bright yellow tobacco. There is an injustice and an impropriety in classing this grade in Europe as " Virginia Strips" which might make the ears of a North Carolinian tingle with shame that no effort had ever been made to free his State from its humiliating insignificance. The present classification of the London market may be retained; but it is right that the agency of the State that almost monopolizes the production of this beautiful and valuable grade should have recognition, and that "North Carolina Brights" take their deserved place alongside of "Virginia Strips." Such recognition would elevate the State from its commercial obscurity; would give it a distinct name and place in the markets of the world; would transfer the attention of buyers and contractors to a new centre of supply; would fill our own markets with foreign orders; would stimulate our own internal transactions; would give new spirit to our manufactories, and would infuse new life into all our business by bringing us in contact with new men and new systems. Importance would be given to our own markets, which is now lost from the practice of dealing through secondary agencies. Importance may be added to our own seaports by giving to them the business which is now absorbed by others. The reproach which attaches to North Carolina—that she is "a strip of land between two States"—would be removed, and she would become recognized in her own right as the most abundant producer of the best tobacco in the United States, as she is the producer of everything else known to the soil and climate of the United States, from Maine to Texas.

In this connection other new sources of supply may be referred to, which promise to become very important in their relation to the crop of brights, adding, like the transmontane section, an unexpected field for the production of that quality of tobacco. These new fields are portions of the counties of Wayne, Lenoir and Sampson—all lying in the eastern belt— and may be much enlarged over present experiment, since the Laurentian formation, overlaid with the quaternary sands, characterizes a very large area.

The Messrs. Borden and Mr. Grant, of Wayne County, have both planted on a large scale—the former having had last year one hundred and five acres in cultivation near Goldsboro. Their success was satisfactory. Their cures of bright were much admired on the Durham and Danville markets, and were assigned a high character. The same may be said of Mr. Parrott, of Lenoir County.

Mr. L. B. Colman, who removed from Person County to Sampson County in 1879, and who bought a farm near Clinton, gives some details of his operations during the crop season of 1880. The soil of his land is a gray, sandy loam, with a growth of long leaf pine and undergrowth of dogwood, sour wood, etc. His experience assures him that the land is very suitable to the production of fine yellow tobacco. Tobacco "yellows" well on the hill and cures readily. Mr. C. cures by flue system. The cultivation is much less laborious than in the upper counties, the ploughing more shallow and much less work required. He had twenty-five acres in cultivation in 1880, but will put in forty acres next year, as he regards his success as unmistakable. He planted on the 29th of April, cutting on the 27th of July. His crop was sold in Danville The quality was superior, the color excellent, and the body good and heavy, comparing favorably with the best from other sections.

Mr. Ashford, of Clinton, had also in 1880 a crop of twenty-five acres in tobacco, and others in the vicinity will engage in the same culture.

In view of the large crop of North Carolina, of the large crop of the United States, of the immense production of the whole world, and also in view of the burdens imposed through revenue systems upon tobacco, the planter is beset with difficulties from which extrication is troublesome. But, as the first step to release, his effort must be to add to the intrinsic value of the article produced. Taxation makes no discrimination in favor of bad tobacco; it is laid with equal hand on good and bad alike, unintentionally, perhaps, putting a premium upon the former and repressing the other by wholesome warning. Common sense teaches the impolicy of persisting in a profitless course, yet every crop is of such character that the bad is out of all proportion to the good, and the average sales of the warehouses show that prices fall twenty-five per cent. below the tax levied per pound on the subject of sale.

The remedy is greatly in the hands of the planter. He must direct his efforts to raise nothing but fine grades. "Against our low grades the world at large can furnish substitutes enough, and at prices that drive us from the market; *for our fine grades there is no substitute.* We are unwise then . if we do not profit by this advantage."*

These fine grades embrace both the bright yellow and the dark manufacturing, both unequalled in their kind, and both dependent for perfection upon culture and cure, and also largely upon subsequent handling. In

* Mr. John Ott, in " Tobacco in Virginia and North Carolina."

culture, both repel gross manures, which are inconsistent with the delicacy of texture and the richness of color characteristic of both in their degree; hence, artificial fertilizers become imperatively necessary in lands of the second year. These fertilizers hold competing repute between the Anchor brand, the Star, the Pacific, Ober's and others, all having their advocates, perhaps with equal justice, variation between them being determined, probably, by local peculiarity.

Culture and cure may be perfect, yet the duties and troubles of the planter are not ended until it is sold, and to do this profitably he must not disregard certain absolute essentials. In getting ready for market, tobacco must be well assorted in respect to size, color and condition. This is a very important matter, because, in mixed grades, the quality of the lowest determines the value of the whole.

Tobacco must not be smoked after it is cured. This is a process which always betrays itself and at once reduces the selling price of the leaf, whatever its color or texture. Transmontane planters have been apt to fall into this practice, owing to the slow introduction of the more approved processes which have come in vogue in late years in the eastern counties.

Tobacco when brought to the warehouses by planters in their wagons, should be brought in as large parcels as possible. Buyers in search of large quantities of like grades prefer to buy in as large parcels as possible, to avoid the necessity of making up their supplies through the accumulation of many small lots. Better prices are paid for large than for small parcels.

Next to assorting, it is important that tobacco be brought to market in "good order," a technicality understood by the farmer, but sometimes neglected in the haste to make sales. There is no instruction that warehousemen are more earnest in impressing than this. Tobacco handled too "high" or too dry is equally objectionable.

Another essential is

Good Seed.

Major R. L. Ragland, of Halifax County, Virginia, one of the most extensive planters of that State, one of the most observing, intelligent and successful cultivators of tobacco, says in a letter addressed to the writer, "the importance of good seed is under-estimated by agriculturists generally," and submits the following valuable views:

"An extended and critical examination of the tobacco fields of Virginia, West Virginia and Maryland, has revealed not only great dissimilarity in the culture, cure and management of this crop, the varying character of the soils and the multitude of the varieties planted, but in far too many instances the lack of adaptation of varieties to soils and types, and the loss consequent from planting degenerated seed of no distinct variety.

"The tobacco seed, like others, is susceptible of improvement or degeneration. It will hybridize, some of our best varieties being the result of cross fertilization of the blooms of our old varieties. These last have been greatly improved by continuous selection—selecting the best as seed plants, and priming off all the seed sprays except the three crown shoots, and clipping the ends of these, thus throwing the whole force of the plant into a small number of seed pods, and taking the seed from the best of these for a series of years.

"In this way pedigree seed are raised that are as sure to transmit their valuable qualities to their product as a thoroughbred animal may be relied upon to transmit his or her fine traits to their offspring.

"The loss consequent upon using inferior seed is nowhere more apparent than in the tobacco crop. The remedy is plain and cheap, for the cost of the best seed to plant a large crop is so small an item that all who desire may, without inconvenience, secure the best.

"The Oronokos and Pryors are good varieties when pure and genuine, and are the sources from which our best plants have come; some of the new are decided improvements upon the old ones. But care must be taken and judgment displayed in the selection, so as to get what is suited to soil and type. The 'Gold Leaf,' which is a hybrid between the Oronoko and Pryor, is a new variety of good promise. It produces an orange or mahogany-colored leaf rather than a lemon color, but will turn out generally a more salable tobacco than either of its progenitors.

"The 'Flannagan,' a high-bred variety of the old 'Narrow Leaf Oronoko,' but broader and finer in texture, is growing in favor, and deservedly, for the best grades of fillers and wrappers.

"The 'White Burley' is a popular filler and cutter, sells well, is much in demand, and deserves trial on all limestone land.

"The mixed varieties in many crops will not cure uniformly nor make a desirable type in any market.

"Select a type that the soil will produce to perfection, and then you may spend labor, means and skill upon it with some assurance of compensation."

CHAPTER XII.

VARIETIES OF TOBACCO, CLASSIFICATION, ETC.

TOBACCO, spread now as a subject of cultivation over all the habitable globe, may be assumed to have acquired characteristics derived from soil, climate, or modes of culture, so as to present as many varieties as there are countries in which it is cultivated. Botanists claim to recognize several species of the plant, and also to ally tobacco by a botanical consanguinity with other plants differing totally in appearance, properties and uses; connecting it with some containing powerful narcotic poisonous properties, such as belladonna, stramonium and hyoscyamus, and also with the innocent tomato and potato. But while several species are recognized, most of the tobacco of commerce comes from the *Nicotiana tabacum*, the common tobacco of the United States. The *Nicotiana rustica* is mostly cultivated in Europe, and also in parts of Asia and Africa, now naturalized in those countries, but coming originally from America. Some of the European tobaccos contain an excess of nicotine. The Levant tobaccos are mild and pleasant, and the Latakia, among the Turkish tobaccos, has a broad yellow leaf of admired fragrance. The Luzon or Manilla tobacco, used for cheroots, is dark and somewhat strong, and is thought to approach the character of the Cuban. This last in exquisiteness of flavor stands first in the esteem of all consumers: used exclusively for cigars, these last were only known to commerce since the opening of the present century. The west end of Cuba, the Vuelta Abajo, produces the most highly prized, combining good color, flavor, and perfect leaves; this tobacco has many classifications not necessary to notice. Another well-known Cuba tobacco is the Yara, grown in the Vuelta Arriba, lying east of the city of Havana.

Other West India Islands, notably Trinidad, which produces a very high-flavored tobacco; Mexico, which makes enough for home consumption; Brazil, which exports largely, and other American States, produce tobaccos, all perhaps with some distinctive features.

The varieties in the United States owe their peculiarities perhaps altogether to soil. The heavy dark tobacco of Kentucky is not essentially different from the bright yellow of North Carolina. The seed leaf of Pennsylvania had the same original. But process of time has brought about changes so great that the superficial eye might infer radical differences. So far the different qualities in North Carolina refer to the same stock. The Oronoko, broad and narrow, and the Silky Pryor, furnish alike the dark mahogany wrappers, the sun-cured fillers, and the bright leaf for wrappers or smokers. Other seed, it is true, have their advocates, but they constitute only sub-varieties. These are the subjects of the active traffic which gives life to the tobacco markets, and they in turn are subjected to classification according to merit.

First, there are the Lugs, which are the ground or inferior leaves, used for smokers and fillers, and which are graded as "common red lugs," "common bright," "good bright," and "fancy bright," the value increasing upwards from the lowest grade.

"Leaf" comes next, and is graded as "common red," "good red," "common brights," and "good brights." This class is used exclusively for fillers.

"Cutting tobacco," a rich, waxy tobacco of medium bright, is graded as "good" and "extra." A very superior article of this class, claimed to be the best in the world, is sold on the Durham (N. C.) market, the product of the adjacent counties, and is now largely used by Blackwell & Co. and E. H. Pogue for "Long Cut."

"Wrappers" are "common," "medium," "good," and "extra, or fancy," and include dark or mahogany wrappers, and the beautiful bright yellow, the subject of such extravagant prices, reaching two dollars and two dollars and a half a pound. This, as its name implies, is used for the covering of the more costly brands of plug tobacco.

THE WAREHOUSE SYSTEM

connects itself naturally with the preceding subject, for in them the terms mentioned are most frequently heard.

Previous to the war, the medium of warehouses to facilitate the business of the planter and buyer was so little known as to be exceptional. Danville in Virginia and Milton in North Carolina had each made a step in the direction of consolidation of the business. But the common practice was to sell to merchants, manufacturers, or buyers, of any class, in modes most convenient to all parties. Much was shipped to factors in Richmond and Petersburg. A great deal was bought by merchants, who were in the habit of keeping annual accounts with the planters, furnishing them with plantation supplies, and making settlements at the end of the year. The war interfered with this system, and the return of peace destroyed it. Neither merchant nor farmer could wait a whole year. The capital of the first could not endure it; the credit of the other was destroyed by the loss of his slave property. He was compelled to live, as it were, from hand to mouth. He had to make frequent small sales to meet family necessities, to pay his laborers or to pay his taxes. He had to find a market often. This demand was met by the opening of sales houses at points on railroads principally, because on railroads could more readily be met the requisitions of the revenue service, the ready and convenient supply of stamps being essential to manufacturers, and these becoming the great patrons of the warehouses. The two have become indispensable complements of each other, as illustrated by Danville, Durham, Reidsville, Winston, Henderson, Oxford, and other points, the centres of the tobacco industry.

The warehouses are invariably large buildings with great floor capacity, and perfectly lighted by ample skylights, so that the color and quality of the tobacco are faithfully exposed. The tobacco, taken from the wagons, where it had been packed down while in "good order," is carefully placed in piles, after having been weighed, each pile of uniform grade. A tag fixed upon a cleft stick is placed upon each pile, on which is the name of the owner of the tobacco, and also the weight. At the hour of sale, outcry is made at each pile, the price bid attached to the tag, and also entered upon a book, and so until the whole is sold. A planter, dissatisfied with a bid, is entitled to "take in" his tobacco. The compensation of the warehousemen is a commission of from 2½ to 3 per cent. on sales. Where there are several warehouses in a market, by arrangement each one is entitled to the first sale in turn. In most of the markets the sales are held daily except in the duller months of the season.

After the sales the buyers are required to remove their purchases within a certain designated time in order that the floors may be clear for another sale. The same rules apply to hogshead or package tobacco as to the loose leaf. The former are shipments from other markets; the latter is the form in which the producer brings his crop to market.

PRIZE HOUSES.

No insignificant feature of a tobacco market are the "prize houses," where tobacco is prepared for shipment or transfer to other markets. On all the markets in North Carolina are standing orders to be filled for Canada, Louisville, Cincinnati, New York, Baltimore, and elsewhere. These prize houses perform the functions necessary to put the tobacco in convenient shape for transportation, which is done in the hogsheads or tierces, in which the leaf, selected according to grade and most carefully and systematically packed, is subjected to heavy pressure by means of screws, and the packages, closely headed up, are ready for their destination.

CHAPTER XIII.

CULTURE AND CURE OF TOBACCO.

IN a matter so important as the management of a crop of such magnitude and value, the writer must rely upon those whose large and successful experience entitles them to be accepted as safe guides by those who are venturing upon a new enterprise. In the older portions of North Carolina and Virginia experience is old enough to confirm the planters in their own plans and systems. In the newly opened tobacco sections experience is what is wanted. Among the many excellent treatises there is none more reliable and ample than that of Major Robert L. Ragland, of Halifax County, Va., a practical farmer on a very large scale, and a gentleman of culture and intelligence.

From Major Ragland is quoted as follows:

Preparation of Plant Beds.

There are two modes for raising plants—in hot-bed or cold frame, or in the open air —one or the other of which has preference according to locality ; the former being more practiced north of forty degrees latitude, while the latter is preferred south of that line. We will here give both, that planters may choose.

The Hot Bed.—Select a southern or southeastern exposure, sheltered on the north, dig and shovel out a space five by twelve feet, or any required length, to the depth of eighteen inches. Place straw to the depth of three or four inches in the bottom of this trench and cover with fresh unrotted manure from the stable to the depth of six or eight inches ; then cover the manure with soil—woods-mould is best—five inches deep, and surround the bed with planks twelve inches wide on north side and six inches wide on the south. These will make a frame over which sections of canvas covering should be placed to keep the bed warm, promote growth and protect the plants. These sections may be made of frames five feet long and three feet wide, with common domestic cloth tacked thereon as a covering, and they answer every purpose as glazed sash, are cheaper and less destructible, and may be used for several years to grow tobacco or horticultural plants. Once used, you will be loth to do without them for the latter purpose. But to return. Tobacco seed is sown on the bed thus prepared at the rate of two teaspoonfuls to a bed five by twelve feet. To sow regularly, mix the seed with a fertilizer, ashes or plaster, and sow in drills three inches apart. A bed twelve feet long will require four sections of canvas covering, which are light and handy and may be put on or off or adjusted at pleasure. When the plants have pretty well covered the surface of the bed, remove the canvas during the day, and only replace them when there is danger of frost, or to keep off the flea-bugs.   There is the advantage of having earlier plants by this mode and perfect security against the plant-bug, which will repay for the additional cost of raising at least a portion of the plants needed for the crop, by this safe mode.

OPEN AIR BEDS.—But there is no question that open air beds are cheapest.   And, where this mode of raising plants is practicable, it is greatly to be preferred for the main supply of plants.   It is a well established opinion that plants raised in the open air stand transplanting better and usually grow off quicker than plants raised in hot-bed or cold frame.

SELECTION OF LOCALITY.— On the selection of a proper locality for a plant bed, and its preparation, largely depends the timely supply of strong healthy plants; without which it is impossible to raise a crop of fine grade. The planter therefore cannot be too careful in choosing a sheltered spot, neither too wet nor too dry, as rich naturally as can be found, and located so as to possess different degrees of moisture.

Go into the woods, original forest if possible, and select a spot near a branch or stream of water, embracing both hillside and flat, and having a southern or southeastern exposure, protected by woods on the north.   Burn over the plat intended for plants, either by the old or new method.   The first consists in placing down a bed of wood on small skids three to four feet apart on the ground, well cleared and raked.   Then fire this bed of wood, and permit it to remain burning long enough to cook the soil brown for half an inch deep.   With hooks, or old hoes fastened to long poles, pull the burning mass of brands a distance of four and a half or five feet, throw on brush and wood, and continue burning and moving the fire until the bed is burned over.   Never burn when the land is wet.   It will require from one and a half to two hours to cook the soil properly.

Or better still: Rake over nicely the plat to be burned, then place down poles from two to four inches in diameter, three and a half to four feet apart, over the entire surface to be burned.   Then place brush thickly over the plat and weight down with wood, over which throw leaves, trash or other combustible material, and set the whole on fire and burn at one operation.

But any mode of burning the plat will suffice, provided that it is effectually done.   After the plat has been burned and has cooled, rake off the large coals and brands, but let the ashes remain, as they are essentially a first-class manure.   Then coulter over the plat deeply or break with grub hoes, and make fine the soil by repeated chopping and raking, observing not to bring the subsoil to the surface, and remove all roots and tufts.   Manure from the stable, hog pen or poultry house, or some reliable commercial fertilizer should be chopped into and thoroughly incorporated with the soil while preparing the bed to be sown.   Experience has demonstrated that it is better to use both.   But beware of using manure containing grass seed.

The judgment of the planter must guide him in the amount of fertilizing material to be applied at this stage; but it were well to remind him that the tobacco plant rarely responds to homœopathic doses of plant food, but that the allopathic usage suits it best.

Sow at the rate of a tablespoonful on every fifty square yards at first sowing, and later resow with a heaping teaspoonful over same surface, to secure a good stand. Injury by frost or bugs may require a third or fourth sowing. Sow a little thick rather than too thin, to meet contingencies and secure a good stand in time.

The best way to sow the seed is to mix them thoroughly with a fertilizer or dry ashes, and sow once regularly over the bed, reserving seed enough to cross sow to promote regularity. The tobacco seed is the smallest of all farm seeds, and consequently requires a light covering. If the seed are sown before the 20th of February, the best way is to firm the surface of the bed by treading it over closely, but if sown later, sweep lightly over with a brush or light rake. Then run surface drains through the bed, with inclination enough to pass off the water. To do this properly run them off four or five feet apart with the foot, then open with a narrow grubbing-hoe to the depth of three or four inches. Then trench deeply around the outside of the bed, to ward off surface water and prevent washing.

MULCHING AND COVERING.—Hog hair whipped fine and scattered over the bed attracts and retains moisture, protects the plants from frost and acts as a manure. There is no better covering for a plant-bed, but unfortunately it is rarely ever in full supply. Fine brush should be placed thickly over the bed, or if not handy, cover with straw or chaff free from grain. A covering of some such material is necessary, or the young plants are likely to be killed by frost or suffer from drought, and they thrive better from some protection.

A STANDING PLANT-BED.—Every planter ought to have a standing plant-bed, which may be secured in the following way: Some time in July or August select one of the best of the old plant-beds, and with hoes shave down the green plants over its entire surface, and cover over thickly with straw or leaves, then place green brush thickly over the bed and weight down with wood. When the whole is dry, some time in the late fall or early winter, set on fire, and thus reburn over the bed. Then chop and rake fine, sow and trench as when first prepared. Repeat the same operation every year, and if the bed is manured properly it will improve and prove a stand-by for many years.

UNBURNED BEDS.—Plants may be raised by going into the forest, selecting a moist rich plat, after raking off the leaves, coultering or chopping the surface fine, manuring heavily and sowing the seed. But such beds rarely hold out well if the season is dry. They never "repeat" well after the first "drawing" like burnt beds; which are more reliable for a successive supply of plants as the season advances.

TIME OF SOWING SEED.—The time for sowing varies with the latitude, variety and season. Between the parallels of 35 and 40 degrees north, compassing the great tobacco belt, beds may be sown any time between the 1st of January and 20th of March, and the sooner the better for the bright grades, which ought to be planted early to mature, ripen and yellow, preparatory to being cured early in the fall, when more successful curings are usually made. Yellow tobacco ought to be planted out in May, but June plantings usually do best in heavy dark grades. The planter will consult his interest by sowing at the proper time to suit the grade he desires to raise.

Plants set out after the 10th of July rarely pay for growing and handling, and if not planted by that time it will be wise to plant the hills in peas, potatoes or something else.

HASTENING THE GROWTH OF PLANTS.—As soon as the plants become "square," *i. e.*, have four leaves, you may begin to force their growth if necessary. Nothing is better at this stage of their growth than to apply dry stable manure, rubbed fine and sowed over the bed, applying at the rate of five bushels to every one hundred square yards. Be sure to have it dry and fine, and apply when the plants are dry. This is a favorable time to apply a good fertilizer, and the best time to apply it is during a shower, or when it is apparent that one is impending.

LOOK OUT FOR THE "FLEA BUG."—If the "fly," as it is called, begins to devour the young plants, apply plaster in which rags saturated with kerosene oil have lain for a few hours, covering the plants with the plaster, if necessary, to keep the little pests from devouring them. Repeat the application after every rain unless the flies have left.

A covering of green cedar brush has driven off the fly when other remedies failed, and saved the plants. If the flies are numerous, the planter can save his plants only by vigilant and constant attention. Hard burning, early and thick sowing, liberal and frequent applications of manure, are the best safeguards, which rarely fail to reward the planter with an early and full supply of stocky plants, and with some left for his less provident neighbors.

SELECTION OF SOIL, PREPARATION AND MANURING.

The tobacco plant thrives best in a deep, mellow, loamy soil, rich or made so with manures. The subsoil ought to be sufficiently porous to permit the water falling on the surface to pass downward readily, and not to accumulate to drown and stagnate.

If old land is selected, it ought to be fallowed deep in the fall or early winter, that the frosts may pulverize it. Turn under, if possible, some coarse farm manure, for its decay will greatly help to loosen the soil, while furnishing pabulum for the crop. As a coarse manure for yellow tobacco, nothing is better than wheat straw turned under in the fall and winter. The plants rarely fail to ripen yellow in color on land thus treated.

In the early spring more manure may be applied, but it is better that this should come from the compost heap. Follow the application of the compost with one-horse turning ploughs, *crossing* the previous ploughing, turning not exceeding four or five inches deep—about half the depth of the first ploughing. Then, just before it is time to plant, run double-shovel ploughs over the lot, *crossing* the previous furrows, and follow with harrow or drag, *crossing* again to make thoroughly fine. These repeated ploughings, *crossing each time every previous one*, never fail, if the work is done when the land is in proper condition, to put it in proper tilth.

Let the planter remember that "a good preparation is half cultivation," and not stop until the land is in proper condition.

Having put the land in nice "order," lay off the rows with a shovel plough three feet three inches apart, and follow, drilling along the furrow some reliable tried fertilizer at the rate of some one hundred and fifty to three hundred pounds per acre, according to the natural strength of the soil and the quantity of manure previously applied. Then follow with one-horse turning ploughs, lapping four furrows on the fertilized trench, and when finished in this manner your lot is ready to be planted, when the beds have been "patted" with hoes, with "pats" two feet ten inches apart, to mark points for setting the plants.

New ground, or old field that has grown up and been cut down, will require different preparation from old smooth land. But on the former our best brights are raised. Any preparation that will put the soil in fine condition, clear of roots, tufts and trash, is all that is required. Experience teaches that if land is cut down two or three years previous to its being prepared for tobacco, it greatly facilitates the preparation and helps its fertility. Much of the vegetable material both in and upon the soil rots, the roots break easily, and the soil is altogether lighter and finer.

While it is economy to dispense with the hand hoe in making hills on old land—the plough doing all the work as it ought, when it can be well done—yet, on stumpy, rooty and rough land, the hoe is indispensable in the preparation of a hill as it should be made to receive the plant. But before the hills are made it may be well, unless the soil is naturally rich, and such is not often the case with soils best adapted to yellow tobacco, to apply some fertilizing material to hasten forward the plants and mature them properly and early. Here commercial fertilizers have done and are doing their best work. Bulky, coarse manures often do more harm than good on new and puffy soils. The smaller the bulk and the more concentrated the fertilizing elements, the more readily they are appropriated and assimilated by the plants, if of the right material and in the most available form. Nitrogen, phosphoric acid, potash, lime and soda are most necessary for the tobacco plant, and a fertilizer which supplies the relative quantity of each will never fail to show good effects therefrom, if the rainfall is sufficient to quicken their action.

MODE OF APPLYING FERTILIZERS.—Planters differ in the manner of applying fertilizers, whether in the hill, drill or broadcast. That the same quantity will go further and produce larger results the first year for the quantity used when applied in the hill or drill, is generally conceded. But advocates for broadcasting claim that when the crop to which the fertilizer is applied is to be followed by another in quick succession—to be sown in wheat as soon as the tobacco is removed—then broadcasting is best, for reasons which seem too apparent to need explanation.

Having prepared the land for hilling, apply the fertilizer by whichever mode the planter prefers, and in such quantity as the natural strength of the soil indicates, laying off the rows three feet three inches apart, and make the hills about two feet ten inches distant from centre to centre. Mark the measure on the hoe handle, and require the hillers to apply it frequently as a guide. The rows should be wider apart than the hills, to afford proper cultivation without breaking and bruising the plants at the final ploughing, a matter of no small importance, as the least blemish on a fine leaf nearly destroys its value as a wrapper.

PLANTING.—Having prepared the hills, you are ready to plant any time after the first of May. Planting is often most effectually done when the hills are being made in May, and the land is moist with the winter's sap, by planting in the afternoon the hills made the same day. If properly planted, very few of the plants will fail to live. Observe to draw the plants one by one from the bed, and handle so as not to bruise them. It is a waste of time and plants to set out very small plants, but wait until they are of proper size—the largest leaves about two and a half to three inches wide. Put a basket of plants in the hands of a boy or girl, who drops a plant on each hill, dropping in one or two rows according to age or expertness. The men follow, with each a planting peg made of hard wood, six inches long, one and a quarter inch in diameter at large end, and tapering to a point. Each planter takes a "hand-plant" to start with (unless the dropper has learned to drop two plants on the first hill), and pushing his planting peg some two inches into the hill, withdraws the peg, inserts the plant, and by a dexterous movement of the peg and the knuckles of the left hand, closes the dirt gently but compactly around the roots. He then picks up the plant on the hill as he moves forward, and by the time he reaches the next hill has adjusted the plant in his hand to insert into the hole in the next hill. Thus the "hand-plant" facilitates the work. Try it and you will be convinced. There is art in planting properly, as is shown in the increased number of living monuments that test superior work. But why enter into such minute details? say some. That you may start right, shun the errors of inexperience, and practice at the start the best methods as demonstrated by successful practice.

If the soil is dry when the hills are made, then it will require a "season" for planting. The best come with showers. It is not well to plant soon after a soaking rain, but wait until the land settles. If the plants are good, seasons favorable, and the planting well done, very few will die, if transplanted before the 10th of July. After that time all is uncertainty. Hence the importance of getting a stand before that time.

After planting over, it will be necessary to replant from time to time as seasons occur, embracing every opportunity to fill up the missing hills. If cut-worms are troublesome, hunt for and destroy every one as far as possible, for it is useless to put a plant in a hill where one of these pests has taken up quarters, and expect it to live and grow.

CULTIVATING.—It is important to commence cultivation soon after planting, to loosen the soil and start the plants growing. Just at this point many planters fail to do their duty, which no subsequent work can atone for. Early, rapid and thorough cultivation is necessary to produce first-class goods. If the preparation has been thorough, thrice ploughing, followed each time with the hand hoe, will suffice for the crop.

For the first ploughing, no implement is better than the wing coulter, the next best the cultivator. The second ploughing may be effactually done with the turning plough or cultivator; if grassy, use the first. The last ploughing is most effectually done with three furrows with the single shovel —a furrow on each side, then splitting the middle with the third and last furrow.

Never "scrape down" tobacco with the hoe without putting back on hill or bed as much dirt as is scraped down. This will prevent baking, and save many plants, should a dry spell follow the hand hoe working.

Any process which stirs the soil effectually and often and keeps the plants free from grass and weeds, will constitute good cultivation, no matter how or with what implement done. Old land will require more work in cultivation than new, and dark grades more than bright. Short singletrees should be used after the plants are half grown, to prevent tearing and breaking the leaves.

The yellow grades should be cleared of grass and weeds before the first of August, and not ploughed thereafter; but the hoes may be used at any time to clear out the crop till the leaves commence graining. The longer tobacco is ploughed the later the plants will be in ripening, therefore the importance of giving early and thorough cultivation. Any one who can raise good cabbage ought to know how to cultivate tobacco, as the cultivation is very similar.

PRIMING AND TOPPING.

Under this head there is a wide difference of opinion. Breaking off the small and inferior leaves of the plant near the ground is called "priming," which operation is done along with the "topping," if done at all. There are advantages for and against priming, but all resort to topping—plucking out the seed bud and adjacent small leaves with the thumb and finger.

Some contend that pulling off the lower leaves saps the plants and retards growth, if the weather is dry. That permitting the lower leaves to remain on the stalk protects the upper ones from sand and grit, makes them cleaner and therefore more salable. On the other hand it is contended by some that by pulling off the lower leaves, which are generally useless, the remaining leaves receive more nutriment and contain more wax, oil and gum. That the lower leaves harbor worms and make the worming process more tedious.

It is best to wait until a considerable number of plants begin to button for seed before commencing to top. Topping should be the work of experienced and trusty hands—men who can top, leaving any required number of leaves on a plant without counting. The secret of this—no longer a secret to the initiated—is, that the topper soon learns to know that counting the bottom leaf and the leaf that hangs over it in the third tier going upward, makes *nine* leaves, including both top and bottom leaves. Fixing this in his mind the topper has only to add to or deduct from this *index leaf* marking *nine*, to leave any desired number of *leaves* on each plant with certainty and without counting. Young man, if you don't know how, get some old negro to show you. Topping you will find is a slow business if you have to count the leaves on all the plants topped. If the plants are not " primed " then the " bottom " leaf must be fixed by the eye, looking upward for the leaf in third tier which hangs over it to catch the cue as before. If priming is done, don't err in pulling off too many leaves. No regular rule can be given, so the planter must judge for himself. The reason given for waiting until many plants are ready to be topped is mainly that more plants may ripen together and be ready for the knife at the same time. This is an advantage that applies with strong force to all tobacco intended for flue curing.

The number of leaves to be left on each plant varies according to the time the work is done, early or late, the appearance and prospective development of the plant, the season, whether propitious or unfavorable, strength of the soil and amount of fertilizing material applied. On medium soils, in ordinary seasons, the first topping should be from ten to thirteen leaves—rarely more—for brights. For sweet fillers from nine to ten, and for dark rich shipping from eight to nine leaves are enough. As the season advances reduce the number of leaves accordingly ; remembering that quality more than quantity regulates returns.

WORMING AND SUCKERING.

Many devices have been resorted to in order to lessen the number and mitigate the ravages of the horn-worm, but the lack of general and continued efforts from year to year has brought only partial relief. Some years they come in great numbers, and despite the best efforts of the planter, seriously damage his crop. Perhaps the next year they are few and give him no trouble. It is the nature of this insect to raise at least two broods during the year. The hawk-moth or tobacco fly usually makes its appearance in Virginia in the month of May. The eggs, deposited by the first moths, hatch out in from five to seven days, larvæ or worms. The worm sheds its outer skin twice before it gets its growth. The growing stage of the worm lasts from twenty-five to thirty days, and after it has attained its growth, it gorges itself a few days longer, and then crawls or burrows into the ground, where it soon passes into the pupa state ; and after some twenty-three or twenty-five days from the time of its crawling into the ground the pupa sends forth a moth to lay more eggs and hatch out more worms. Each moth is capable of laying on an average two hundred eggs. So that for every moth in May we may reasonably expect at least one hundred worms of the first brood; and if none of these are destroyed but all allowed to change to moths and these latter to raise a horde of worms, what wonder that the second brood sometimes appears in such countless numbers as to defy all efforts to destroy them before they have ruined the crop. Every moth ought to be destroyed as they appear; and this may be done to great extent by injecting a few drops of sweetened Cobalt into the flowers of the Petunia, Honey-Suckle or Jamestown (Jimpson) weed, which will give them their final quietus. But this hunt for the moth is not general, and if it were some would escape. But if every planter would wage a war of extermination on the *first brood* of worms— unfortunately a thing rarely done—they would never appear in such unconquerable hordes later in the season. The suckers should be pulled off every week as they appear, and ought never to be permitted to get over two inches long ; for if permitted to grow large they abstract much that would otherwise go to perfect a rich, silky leaf. No planter need expect a crop of fine grade who does not pull off the suckers while small, and prevent the horn worms from riddling the leaves.

Cutting and Housing.

Do not be in a hurry to begin cutting your tobacco until it is ripe, and enough fully and uniformly ripe to fill a barn. A thin butcher or shoe knife, well sharpened, and wrapt with a soft cloth around the handle and extending an inch along the blade, will do the work effectually and be easy to the hand. Try it. Put knives into the hands of experienced cutters only—men who know ripe tobacco, and will select plants uniform in color and texture, and will cut no other. Have your sticks all ready in the field, and placed in piles convenient - sticking a stick vertically in the ground over each pile that they may be more easily found when wanted. Pine sticks, rived three-fourths of an inch by one and one-fourth inch, and four and one-half feet long, drawn smooth, are best.

Start together two cutters and one stick-holder,—the cutters carrying two rows each and the stick-holder walking between them. The cutter takes hold of the plant with his left hand at the top near where the knife enters the stalk ; with his right he splits the stalk down the centre (observing to guide the knife so as not to sever the leaves,) to within three inches of the point he intends to sever the stalk from the hill ; and as the knife descends, his left hand follows the slit or opening, and when the plant is severed from the hill, by a dexterous movement of the left hand the plant is straddled across the stick in the hands of the holder. When the stick has received about six medium plants, if intended for brights, it is ready to go to the barn, either carried by hand if near, or hauled on a wagon if distant. If it is necessary to use the wagon, prepare a bed sixteen feet long to hold three coops or piles, on which place the tobacco as cut, and after placing twenty-five or thirty sticks of cut tobacco on each coop, drive to the barn to be unloaded.

Tobacco suitable for brights is best handled in this way, as it is bruised less than if handled by any other mode. Try it, planters ; and *know* for yourselves. Very heavy tobacco will break less if, after being cut by the above mode, the sticks are placed gently on the ground and the plants allowed to wilt before being removed to the barn. But tobacco of medium size bruises less to handle it without wilting. Cutting and housing by this mode, you never have any sun-burned tobacco. For brights, it has been found best to commence curing at once, as soon as the barn can be filled.

Curing "Bright Yellow."

There are two modes for curing yellow tobacco : one with charcoal and the other with flues. The first is the primitive mode, but is gradually giving place to the latter, which is cheaper and more efficient, and is being adopted by most of our best planters. The chief agent in either mode is heat—a dry, curing heat—to expel the sap from the leaves, stems and stalks of the plants, and catch the color, *yellow*, next to Nature's color, green, and to *fix* it indelibly. This is the *science* of curing *yellow* tobacco. There are seven prismatic colors—that of tobacco occupying the middle of the prism. By the process of nature, leaves in drying descend in color from green, first to yellow, then orange, then red, and finally lose all color as they go to decay. Now a quick dry heat, so regulated as to dry out the leaf and catch the yellow and fix it, is the *modus operandi* of curing fancy tobacco.

A barn containing seven hundred sticks of green tobacco, six medium plants on each stick, holds along with the tobacco four thousand five hundred to five thousand pounds of water, which must be expelled in from eighty-five to one hundred hours.

Charcoal produces an open, dry heat, well suited for the purpose ; but its preparation is costly, its use tedious, dirty and laborious, and it deposits a black dust on the leaf that is objectionable. With flues constructed of stone or brick, and covered with sheet iron, or patent ones with furnace and pipes, the wood is burned as cut in the forest or old field, and the whole process of curing is less costly and less laborious, and the tobacco cured therewith free from dust, and has a sweeter flavor. The flue process possesses so many advantages over all other modes of curing tobacco, is so safe, if properly constructed, and free from smoke, that when its merits become better known it will come into general use and supersede all other modes.

The first step in curing is called the STEAMING OR YELLOWING process. Medium tobacco will require from twenty-four to thirty hours steaming at about ninety degrees to yellow sufficiently; but tobacco with more or less sap, larger or smaller, will require a longer or shorter time to yellow. Here the judgment of the curer must be his guide. Inexperienced planters would do well to procure the services of an expert curer, if they have tobacco suitable for fine yellow. The planter saves in the enhanced value of his crop many times the money paid to the curer, and besides, by close attention, he may learn in one season to cure well himself. Theory alone, however good, and directions, however minute, will not do here, but it is *practice* that must qualify one to cure well.

When it is remembered that no two plants are exactly alike, no two barns precisely similar in every particular, and that the weather may change every hour, is it reasonable that a fixed programme can be followed for every curing with any reasonable hope of success? The experienced know better. On work so variable, only general directions can be given.

The next step is called FIXING THE COLOR. When the tobacco is sufficiently yellowed, the best leaves of a uniform yellow, and the greener ones of a light pea-green color, it is time to advance the heat to one hundred degrees; observing the leaves closely to detect sweating, which will soon redden and spoil the color, unless driven off. To do this, open the door and let it stand open, and if after an hour or more the sweat has not disappeared, open a space between the logs on opposite sides of the barn to let in more air, and permit it to remain open until the tobacco has dried off all appearance of the sweat. Right at this point more curings are spoiled than at any other stage of the process. It may be well to remember what is a fact, that at least five curings are spoiled by proceeding too *fast*, to one failure from going too *slow*. Now stick a pin here.

But to go back to the barn where we have just dried the leaf, and where the thermometer indicates a fall of five to ten degrees—but this need not concern the curer to put him out of hope, for a little cooling under the circumstances was necessary—we close up the opening and raise the heat to one hundred degrees. But a skillful curer detects the first indications of sweat and prevents it by regulating the heat.

Keep the heat at one hundred degrees for four hours, and then advance two and a half degrees every two hours until one hundred and ten degrees are reached. Here you have reached the most critical point in the difficult process of curing bright tobacco. The condition and appearance of the tobacco must now be the curer's guide. No one can successfully cure tobacco until he can distinguish the effects of too much or too little heat in the appearance of the leaf. Too little heat, in fixing the color, operates to stain the *face* side of the leaf a dull brown color, and is called "sponging," and may be known to the novice by its appearance only on the *face side* of the leaf. Too much heat reddens the leaf, first around the edge and then in spots, which are visible on *both sides*. Now, to prevent sponging on the one hand and spotting on the other, is the aim of the experienced curer. No definite time can be laid down to run from one hundred and ten to one hundred and twenty degrees. Sometimes four hours will suffice, then again eight hours is fast enough. While it is usual at this stage to advance about five degrees every two hours for medium tobacco, the condition of the tobacco often indicates to the practised eye the necessity for slower or faster movement. But it is safe not to advance above one hundred and ten degrees until the tails begin to curl up at the ends. Arrived at one hundred and twenty or one hundred and twenty-five degrees, this is the CURING process. The heat should remain at or near these figures until the leaf is cured, which will require from six to eight hours, according to the amount of sap in the leaf to be expelled. When the leaf appears to be cured, advance five degrees every hour up to one hundred and seventy degrees and remain until stalk and stem are thoroughly cured. To run above one hundred and eighty degrees is to endanger scorching the tobacco, and perhaps burning barn and tobacco.

To recapitulate:

First. Yellow process,   90 degrees, from 24 to 30 hours.
Second. Fixing Color,   100 degrees, 4 hours.
"   "   "   100 to 110, 2½ degrees every 2 hours.
"   "   "   110 to 120, 4 to 8 hours.
Third. Curing the leaf,   120 or 125, 6 to 8 hours.
Fourth. Curing stalk and stem, 125 to 170, 5 degrees an hour. And continue at one hundred and seventy degrees until stalk and stem are thoroughly killed and dry, which usually requires from twelve to fifteen hours.

After curing, as soon as the tobacco is sufficiently soft to move, you may run it up in the roof of the barn and crowd it close, or if the barn is needed for other curings, the tobacco may be carried to the storage barn or bulked down in any dry house on the premises. But be sure that nothing is bulked with green stalks or swelled stems, for if such are placed down in bulk it will be sure to heat and utterly ruin.

ORDERING.

If, after the tobacco is cured, the weather remains dry and it fails to get soft readily, so that it can be moved, it may be brought in order in the following way: Place green bushes with the leaves on over the floor and sprinkle water over them copiously; if the tobacco is very dry and the atmosphere contains but little moisture, and if the weather is cool, a little fire kindled in the flues will assist in making the tobacco soft. Straw wet or made so will answer the same purpose. If the weather is damp there will be no necessity to use either straw, brush or water. But when it is necessary to use any means to order tobacco, it is best to apply them in the afternoon, that the tobacco may be removed the next morning.

If the weather remains warm and damp or rainy, tobacco that remains hanging will be apt to change color unless dried out by flues or charcoal. When this becomes necessary, build small fires at first and raise the heat gradually.

STRIPPING.

Tobacco should never be stripped from the stalks except in pliable order, and the leaves on every plant should be carefully assorted and every grade tied up separately. Usually there will be three grades of leaf, assorted with reference to color and size, and two of lugs. Of leaf tie six to eight leaves in the bundle, and of lugs eight to ten. As fast as you strip either, hang the "hands" on sticks—twenty-five to each stick—and hang up or bulk down in two layers, the heads of hands or bundles facing outward. The latter mode is best if you intend to sell in winter order, *loose* on the warehouse floors. If bulked down, watch frequently to see that it does not heat. If the bulk becomes warm it must be broken up, aired and rebulked, or hung up if too soft. It is safer always to hang up as soon as stripped, unless you design to sell soon, and strike down in "safe keeping order" in spring or summer. It is considered in "safe order" when the leaf is pliable and the stem will crack half way down from the tie.

PACKING.

If you sell loose, deliver in large uniform piles; such will cost less and your tobacco bring more in price. But to sell in a distant market pack in tierces—half hogsheads make the best and cheapest—to weigh about four hundred pounds net, taking care not to press the tobacco so as to bruise it or pack it too closely together. The best leaf is wanted for wrappers, and it must open easily when shaken in the hand. Pack one grade only in each tierce, uniform in color and length; but if it becomes necessary to put more than one grade in a tierce, place strips of paper or straw between to mark and separate them. Pack honestly, for honesty is always the best policy.

If your tobacco is fine, sound and nicely handled, you'll have the satisfaction of getting at the least a remunerating price for it, although poor and nondescript stock may be selling for less than the cost of production. The world is now full of low grades of tobacco. We must plant less surface, manure heavier, and cultivate and manage better, if we would get better prices.

Construction of Barn with Furnace and Flue.*

The site selected for the barn should, when practicable, be ground that slopes to the east with an inclination of two feet in twenty, in order to admit the furnaces readily, which should always be placed in the eastern side of the barn, for the reason that during the curing season the prevailing winds are from the west. When there are more barns than one, they should, for the convenience of moving and storing the tobacco after it is cured, be grouped together, but not nearer to each other than 100 feet.

The dimensions of the barn is next to be determined. I am aware that the size approved by the majority of fine curers is only sixteen feet square, divided by tier-poles into four equal compartments or rooms, each room having perpendicularly only four firing tiers in the body including the joists. Another convenient size, although not so generally approved, is one twenty feet square, similarly divided into five rooms with five firing tiers to each. The comparative housing capacity of the two is about as four is to seven, the smaller barn holding 352 sticks and the larger 650 sticks, when placed one foot apart. Between them the reader is left to his own choice, while in point of economy I must decide in favor of the larger size, it being obvious that the size of the barn can have nothing to do with the success of a cure, provided always that the capacity of the furnace and flue is in proportion to the size of the barn, which in one twenty feet square is easily attainable.

The body of the barn should be always of logs of an average thickness of six inches, notched down closely, the ground sills being much larger and invariably of oak and well underpinned. The roof should be framed and what is called square, and covered with shingles or two foot boards, the board roof being preferable if the barn is one for curing only, while the shingle roof is to be preferred if it is one for storing as well as curing. The gables should be tightly weather-boarded, each having a small window with shutters just below its centre, together with a small opening at its upper angle, which serve as escapes for the heated vapor.

When the barn has been raised a height of five feet, a set of six tier-poles should be laid on horizontally, resting upon the northern and southern walls of the barn, and dividing it accurately into five equal parts, the two outside ones resting against its eastern and western walls. This first set are called the ground tiers, and are not used in curing but only in unloading and hoisting the tobacco. These, like all the other tier-poles to be used, had best be of pine, and of an average thickness of four inches, to prevent their springing and sagging while the barn is being filled. As fast as three additional logs to each wall have been raised, another set of six tier-poles should be laid on as before, and directly above the first, and so on until the sixth set have been laid on, which serve also for the joists. Directly above and in line with these joists, rafters should be placed when the roof is being

* R. B. Davis, Catawba Co., N. C.

framed, upon which collar-beams are to be nailed two and a half feet above each other, which also serve for tier-poles, thus adding about one and a half full tiers to each room. When completed, the walls should contain about twenty logs each, including plates, and be about sixteen feet high. And after they have been roofed they should be tightly chinked and daubed with mud, inside and out, into which a sufficient quantity of lime, when convenient, should have been worked to make it adhere well, the mud being laid in with a trowel. The object is to have the walls practically air-tight, whatever fresh air that may be needed in curing being admitted from below. In the northern and southern walls of the barn, and at their centres, closely fitting doors four feet square should be cut.

Framed buildings, although ceiled, will not answer for curing for the reason that they cannot be heated sufficiently.

The directions which remain to be added have reference to flue-curing, as contradistinguished from coal-curing, the latter having pretty well gone out of use, because of its greater cost and discomfort to the curer, as well as the inferior quality of the work done by that process, the flavor and color of the coal-cured leaf being invariably injured by the soot of the burning charcoal.

And the flue to which I have reference is the well known Smith patent, which is constructed on the principle of the return draft, and with the model of which most tinners are familiar. It communicates with two furnaces built in the corners of the barn, by pipes laid along three of its walls, and one foot from them, and uniting in a single return pipe through its centre. The piping should be gently and uniformally elevated, say 6 inches in 20 feet, so that there shall not be more than eighteen inches perpendicular between the points where it leaves the furnaces and where it comes out through the wall of the barn. If greater elevation is given, the draft will be increased, but at the expense of too much heat, which will be wasted through the smoke-stack, which is a short elbow joint fitted on the outer end of the return pipe.

For a barn of the given dimensions, the piping should be of No. 24 iron (except the two joints which enter the furnaces, and which should be of No. 18,) and not less than 12 inches in diameter, 15 inches being still better—the one I use is 13 inches. Such a flue is portable and easily carried from one barn to another.

There are other flues of later invention which claim to be superior to the Smith—of them I know nothing except that in such things the latest is commonly the best.

The construction of the furnaces remains to be noticed. If the ground plot is properly inclined it will be necessary to remove only a single log in order to admit them, which should be done by sawing it out 4 inches from the corners. The furnaces should be of brick or fireproof stone, 5 feet long, and project 18 inches outside the barn. Their walls should be a thickness of 2 bricks, and built 2 feet apart and 18 inches high, and arched over with the thickness of a single brick. Their outside walls should be laid 4 inches from the walls of the barn, the intervening spaces being filled with dry earth, while the space between the furnaces should be underpinned to the first log. Care should be taken that no part of the furnace comes in contact with the wood of the barn, and for that reason, as well as to moderate the heat with fresh air, small openings should be left just above the arches. The inside ends or throats of the furnaces should be sloped or slightly drawn together in order to give a good fit to the pipes, which should be inserted some 6 inches above their floors, after which all cracks should be closed with soft mud.

With the view of giving the flue its greatest heating capacity, I have directed that the pipes should be laid only 1 foot from the walls of the barn. To do so with safety to the barn, a thin false wall should be laid between them and the ground sills for a length of 6 feet from the furnaces, that being about as far as the pipes are reddened by heat. This and every other necessary precaution should be taken against burning the barn, which often happens, but always from inexcusable carelessness.

The flue should be taken to pieces and burnt out with straw whenever it begins to choke with soot.

It takes from two to three cords of wood for a single curing, which should be dry and one-half pine.

When all else is completed, a shelter, the length of the barn and 8 feet deep, should be put above the furnaces.

CHAPTER XIV.

CIGAR TOBACCO.

WHILE North Carolina stands pre-eminently the first in the production of bright yellow tobacco, and second only to Virginia in the dark chewing tobaccos, she has had to yield without a contest to the superiority of Connecticut, Pennsylvania, and Ohio, in a cigar tobacco partaking largely of the aromatic flavor of the envied product of Cuba. It is, indeed, related on the authority of Prof. Horsford, of Harvard University, that on a visit to a large cigar factory in Havana, he was honored with the gift of a few cigars made for the especial use of the Emperor Louis Napoleon, and was informed that the leaf of which they were composed was from North Carolina. Without doubting the statement, it is certain that there was a rare exception to general character, our tobacco being unequalled for the pipe or the cigarette, but wanting in the flavor so exquisite in the genuine Havana.

This flavor the tobaccos of the States above-named have in a large degree. Cannot the same be produced in North Carolina and in Virginia, so favored by soil and climate for the perfection of all other grades?

If it were a question of latitude simply, the answer might be given at once. The mountain counties by their altitude would fall along the isothermal line of Pennsylvania and Connecticut, and develop an identity of character. But experiment has not justified such conclusion. Those mountain counties *do* produce the bright yellow in admirable perfection, but they *will not* respond to the demand for cigar tobacco.

It has been shown that it is not a question of climate, but one of soil; that portions of the same county, geologically dissimilar, will be unlike in their products, and that Nature will not yield to the most persevering skill of the cultivator when she has definitely fixed the boundaries between one formation and another. Therefore, dark wrappers and fillers must be the result of one soil, bright yellow of another. This is the rule, from which there is little exception. If another variety of tobacco is sought to be added, its characteristics must be studied, and the soil on which it flourishes be submitted to analysis that its geological composition may be determined.

As the Laurentian system is proven to be the favored one for bright yellow tobacco and the Huronian for darker qualities, so the Triassic may be accepted as the home of cigar tobacco, at least in the United States. Prof. Kerr, in Vol. 1. of his Geological Survey of North Carolina, assigns it the lowest grade in the Mesozoic (middle life) system, "a system," he says, "very scantily represented on the Atlantic slope, being limited to the narrow tracts of sandstones, with shales and conglomerates, so well known in the Connecticut valley, which extends also, with few interruptions, from the Hudson River, in southeastern New York, to the upper border of South Carolina. . . . But the important feature of it here (North Carolina) and Virginia, is the occurrence of extensive and valuable seams of coal, and while the strata of this series are generally poor in fossils elsewhere on the Atlantic slope, there have been found in this latitude many new and interesting organic forms, both vegetable and mineral."

It is in this belt that the cigar tobacco attains so much importance in Pennsylvania and Connecticut. Prof. Jed Hotchkiss, topographical engineer, of Virginia, in a letter addressed to Mr. John Ott, Secretary of the Virginia Fertilizer Company, calls attention to the matter as follows : " Knowing that the famous 'seed leaf' (cigar) tobacco of the Connecticut valley is grown on the soils overlying the Triassic, or New Red Sandstone rocks, as also in Lancaster County, Pennsylvania, it has often occurred to me that a similar leaf might be reared upon the same formation in Virginia, where these rocks cover an area of about 1,600 square miles." And Prof. Hotchkiss presents a map showing the occurrence of this formation whereever it appears. • What has been attempted in Virginia under such enlightenment is not known. The knowledge of so important a fact should not be lost. It concerns North Carolina to know if such formation exists within her territory, and if so, to subject it to intelligent tests.

The answer is, that there are *two* such formations : " the smaller or Dan River belt, from two to four miles wide, following the trough-like valley of that stream (about N. 65° E.) for more than 30 miles, to the Virginia line ; the other, or Deep River belt, extending in a similar trough 5 to 15 miles wide, (and depressed 100 to 200 feet below the general level of the country) from the southern boundary of the State, in Anson County, in a N. E. direction to the middle of Granville County within 15 miles of the Virginia line."* Or, reversing directions, beginning about half a mile south of Oxford, and stretching towards the southwest with varying width, and extending across the State to the South Carolina line, interrupted only once by the Pee Dee river valley and its flanking hills, for a few miles. The North Carolina railroad enters this formation about five miles west of Durham, and emerges ten miles from Raleigh. Durham, therefore, already in commanding relations to the other varieties of tobacco, may become the centre also of an entirely new and lucrative industry. For it is not to be questioned that, if "seed leaf" owes its existence to the elements of this special formation, the influence of a lower latitude must have a decisive effect in heightening flavor, as well as extending the season of cultivation.

A wide prospect is opened to intelligent enterprise and industry. Success would revolutionize industries, would bring into culture thousands of acres given over to unproductiveness, and would give the favored section,

---

* Kerr's Geological Survey, p. 141.

if not a monopoly of, at least a large control over an article now almost the subject of monopoly.

The treatment of this variety of tobacco is so different from that which regulates Southern practice, that copious extracts from a treatise by A. C. Libhart, of Lancaster, Pa., are given.

The preliminary sections on Soils and Situation and Seed Beds are omitted, because experience on those points is almost the same everywhere. The extracts begin with

VARIETIES.

The best variety for cultivation in a high northern latitude is the Connecticut seed-leaf, as it ripens two weeks earlier than most any other variety, cures and colors better, and commands the highest price in the market. The Pennsylvania seed-leaf outstrips the Connecticut in size and weight, but owing to its requiring a longer time to mature in, is not so well adapted to climates north of 41° or 42°.

PREPARATION OF THE SOIL.

The manure should be spread and plowed down several weeks before it is intended to plant. There is scarcely any limit as to the quantity of manure that may be put to the acre, it seeming that the richer the ground is the larger will be the tobacco. As an instance verifying this fact, a gentleman in this place raised the past season on a half-acre of land fourteen hundred lbs. of tobacco, of the aggregate value of $230. There was $25 worth of barn-yard manure put upon it at about the rate of fifty cents per one horse load; the average crop in the vicinity was only about twelve hundred lbs. to the acre. After the land is plowed, and a few days before it is intended to plant, the soil should be well worked with a harrow or large cultivator until it is free from lumps or clods, when it is ready for ridging; this is performed with a common plow. Beginning on one side of the field, take a light furrow, so as to throw up a ridge about five or six inches higher than the surrounding surface of the field. When arrived at the end, return another furrow alongside, so that the earth thrown up by the plow unites with that of the former furrow, leaving a ridge apparently about ten inches in height, but really only five or six above the general level. So proceed, making the apex of the ridges three-and-a-half feet apart, until the whole is finished. Measure off the distance of thirty-six inches for the plant on the top of the ridge, with an instrument constructed as follows: Take two strips of board, two-and-a-half feet long and an inch square, make one end of each pointed, then spread them in the form of a pair of compasses, until the points are the desired distance apart, making the other ends lap each other, fasten them, and put a brace across about the middle to keep them stiff; with this instrument one person can go before, and planting one point at a time on the apex of the ridge, measure off rapidly and correctly the place for each plant. Now take a hoe, and at each indentation made by the compasses, cut off about two or three inches in depth of the top of the ridge, and tap it lightly with the back of the hoe this forms a platform or "bench" for the reception of the plant.

TRANSPLANTING.

When the ridge has been thus prepared, one person goes ahead with a basket of plants and drops one on each "bench," another person following and planting as rapidly as possible, as it is injurious to the plant to leave its roots long exposed to the air. In inserting the plant, a hole may be made with a pointed stick, but the most expeditious, as well as the best way, is with the hands. The roots of the plant are carefully inserted, and the earth pressed moderately tight upon them ; care must be taken not to press the delicate heart leaves, for upon their preservation depends the future vigor of the plant. The best time for planting is during a warm, drizzling rain ; but if no such occasion presents itself, when everything is ready, then immediately before or after a shower will do nearly as well. If it is necessary to plant without any rain, it should be done in the evening, and each plant watered slightly. Unless absolutely necessary, never plant when the ground is in the consistence of mud, as the roots are doubled up and stuck together, and there is considerable time lost in starting the plant, if, indeed, it ever becomes vigorous. In taking the plants from the bed, if the earth is not previously well moistened by rain, water the ground sufficiently, so that the plants will come up with some earth attached to the roots; they may be pulled by taking hold and gently doubling up the several large leaves of the plant at once ; they are very nicely raised with a common table fork. After the whole area has been planted, it should be gone over every few days, and such plants as have been destroyed by the cut-worms, or otherwise, replaced by new ones ; if, however, a plant shows signs of remaining vitality, it should not be destroyed, but a new one placed alongside, as it often happens that a plant of the first setting, even though it be injured, will eventually outstrip in growth one of a subsequent planting ; either can be used to advantage in replacing any missing plants at the first hoeing, transplanting them with a large ball of earth to the roots.

CULTIVATION.

When the weeds begin to appear pretty abundantly, and after the plants have made visible growth, a cultivator must be run between the rows, taking care that it does not throw up the earth on the ridges and cover the plants ; a cultivator that can be regulated in width is the best. Hoe down the prominences of the ridges to a level with the plants, and eradicate all weeds that have come up between the leaves of the plants ; also transplant from any double plants to such hills as have become vacant. The plants will now begin to grow vigorously, and require no attention beyond transplanting to fill vacancies, until a new crop of weeds appears, when the cultivator must be again run through, and the plants carefully hoed, fresh earth being drawn up after the weeds have been scraped away. Care must be taken not to hoe too deep close to the plant, as it destroys too many of the fibrous roots which have begun by this time to permeate the soil in every direction. When the weeds and grass have been thoroughly killed by the sun, the shovel-plow or hook may be run between the rows, and following after, uncover such leaves as may have been buried by the earth thrown up by the implement, and hoeing the ridges into an even shape, rather flat upon the top, and rounding off gradually till they meet in the centre between the rows of tobacco, forming a ditch or furrow not too deep, but answering the purpose of a drain. This is all the cultivation it will require, but if the weeds come up between the rows thereafter, it will benefit the tobacco as well as the ground if they are scraped off with a hoe.

Topping.

There can be no stated time for this, as it depends upon the stage of growth in which the plant may be, and the latitude or climate. As a general thing, it should be topped before the seed-buds are visible, for when these appear, the plant has expended most of its vigor, and is no longer able to mature the upper leaves ; and it must be done at least four weeks before the period of heavy frosts. The number of leaves that may be left to a stalk depends upon the quality of the soil; if it be very strong, it will mature twenty or twenty-four leaves, but in general from sixteen to twenty is amply sufficient to leave on a stalk in any situation. In topping, it is better to pinch out enough of the crown of the plant to leave the first two leaves not less than three or four inches long, as they grow more vigorously and mature more rapidly than the small and tender leaves found about the blossom buds. In pinching out the heart of the plant, care must be taken not to break or injure the upper leaves that are left. When topping, the plants intended to produce seed for the following year's crop must be spared ; they should always be chosen with regard to the heaviest, as well as the longest and broadest leafed plants, as weight and size of leaf is the chief consideration of tobacco-growers. The seed-stalks should be left standing until the pods are fully formed and begin to turn brown, when the leaves may be stripped off and saved, and the stalk be spaded up and placed beyond the reach of frost until the seed is fully ripe.

Suckering.

Soon after the tobacco has been topped the "suckers" begin to appear from the junction of every leaf with the stalk ; they must be pinched off as soon as they are large enough to be caught by the thumb and finger, and every new one that appears must be served likewise, for if left they consume much of the nourishment that would otherwise go to the leaves, besides much impairing the process of curing when the stalk is hung up.

CUTTING AND HOUSING.

When the top leaves have attained the size of the lower ones and begin to be dotted with reddish spots, the tobacco is ripe, and ready to be cut off and hung up to cure. There are several methods of hanging up tobacco, but the following two are the best and shortest: First, splitting and hanging it upon laths or poles and leaving it to partially cure in the field. Secondly, nailing it to rails with lathing-nails at once in the shed. The former method, for high northern latitudes, is by far the best, as it will cure in a much shorter time (and thus prevent the destruction of the crop by freezing in the shed) by the drying of the pith of the stalk, which is the main reservoir of moisture. It is performed as follows: Have a chisel about a foot long and three inches broad, the sharp end not beveled on one side but coming to an edge by a gradual taper on both sides (a common tenon saw will do pretty well); place the edge of the chisel in the centre of the stalk upon the end where it has been topped and push it down, guiding it in its course so as not to break or cut off any leaves, to within three or four inches of the ground; the stalk may then be cut off with a hatchet, or with the chisel if it be made pretty strong. The splitting may be done in the morning when the leaves are too brittle to admit of the stalk being cut down, and then, when the sun has sufficiently wilted the leaves, the stalk may be cut and left to lie until it will bear handling without breaking the leaves. The lath being previously prepared, four feet in length, and about an inch in thickness on one edge and one-half inch on the other, and two inches broad (or poles cut in the forest will answer pretty well); then have trestles prepared high enough to allow the stalks to hang suspended without touching the ground, and set far enough apart in the field to admit of the lath reaching from one to another; now place the stalks of tobacco upon the lath (previously laid across the trestles) by slipping them over and down until they will hang perpendicular, and six or eight inches apart, so they will merely touch without crowding too much. It may be left hanging thus exposed to the weather until the leaves are so wilted that the stalks hang apart without touching and the lower leaves begin to dry, when it is taken off the trestles, each lath entire, and laid upon a wagon and hauled to the

SHED OR DRYING-HOUSE.

The shed must be constructed of timbers strong enough to resist storms and should be boarded " up and down." About every three feet one board should be hinged, to readily open and shut. If it is intended to split and lath the tobacco, the inside of the shed must be divided by rails into widths to accommodate the laths, and likewise into tiers, one above the other, far enough apart to allow the stalks to hang from, well separate. The frame of rails and timbers inside the shed, destined to sustain the weight of the tiers of tobacco (which, when green, is exceedingly heavy), should be strongly constructed so as to preclude the possibility of breaking down, for if this should happen to the upper tier, in all probability the whole would be tumbled to the ground. When ready to hang up, beginning at the top tier of the shed, slip on one lath after the other until the whole is filled. The process of nailing it up to rails or strips of board in some respects may be superior to the former method, as the tobacco is more expeditiously secured in the shed and does not require so much handling; but in general there is more tobacco lost by being frozen in the shed than will pay for the difference in time and labor. The stalk should be cut down after the dew is off in the morning and left to wilt. If the sun be very hot the tobacco must be watched that it does not scorch, and if this be found to be the case, it should be thrown in heaps about a foot high and three feet or less in width, and then hauled into the shed. Here it must not be piled more than a foot high, or it will soon heat and spoil. It should be nailed up as rapidly as possible—one person sticking the nail in the pith of the stalk exposed by cutting it off from the ground and shaking it to loosen the leaves, hands it to a second person, who nails it to the rail far enough apart to allow of the circulation of the air throughout. After the crop is in, the doors and shutters should be opened all round, so as to allow a strong draught of air to pass through the tobacco and prevent what is technically called "burning." This is literally nothing more than a partial decomposition of the leaf consequent upon the exclusion of air from passing through it while in the green state, which destroys its quality and texture. When dried it has a blackish brown color and crumbles beneath the touch. When the tobacco is pretty thoroughly cured and during dry weather, when it is very brittle, the high winds that prevail about that season will damage it very much if allowed to blow through the shed. Hence, at such times the shed should be closed on the sides whence the wind comes and opened again when it has ceased to blow. When the leaves are all dry, or after the weather has been severe enough to freeze the remaining green ones, the tobacco is ready to be stripped.

STRIPPING.

At the setting in of a warm, drizzling, wet, foggy spell of weather, the shed must be opened on all sides to allow the damp atmosphere to pervade the whole interior. After the dry leaves have become damp enough to allow handling in any degree without breaking, the stalks must be taken off the lath, or pulled down and laid in heaps about eighteen inches or two feet high and any desired length. If it is not intended to strip it immediately it should be conveyed to a cellar or other apartment where it will remain damp. It should not, however, be suffered to remain longer than two or three days in heaps without examination, as there is sometimes sufficient moisture remaining in the stalks or frozen leaves to create heat and rot the good tobacco. If found to be heating it should be changed about and aired, and be stripped immediately. If found to be drying out, further evaporation may be checked by covering the heaps with damp straw or corn-fodder. Tobacco is usually stripped into two qualities—"ground leaf," or "fillers," and "wrappers." The leaves that lie next the ground, generally from two to four, are always more or less damaged by sand beating on, by the rain and other causes; hence they only command about half the price of the good tobacco or "wrappers." The ground leaves are taken off first and tied up separately in bunches or "hands." This is performed in the following manner: Take off one leaf after another until there is contained in the hand a sufficient number to make a bunch about an inch in diameter at the foot-stalks, which must be kept even at the ends, and, holding the bunch clasped in one hand, take a leaf and wrap it around (beginning at the end of the bunch), confining the end under the first turn, continue to wrap smoothly and neatly until about three inches of the leaf remain, then open the bunch in the middle and draw the remaining part of the leaf through. This forms a neat and compact "hand" that will bear a great deal of handling without coming open. After the ground-leaves have been removed, the good leaves are stripped off and tied up the same as the ground-leaves, with this exception—the leaves of each stalk should be tied in a bunch by themselves to preserve a uniformity in color and size, as tobacco is sold in the market according to color and size. Therefore, if the leaves of a large and a small plant, or of a dark colored and a light one, be tied up together it at once diminishes the appearance and value of the crop.

BULKING.

As soon as a quantity of tobacco is stripped it should be "bulked down," or if intended to be immediately delivered at the packing-house, put up in bales. A place to bulk it in should be damp enough to prevent the tobacco from becoming dry, and not damp enough to cause it to mold. A platform raised a few inches from the ground, and open to let the air circulate under, must first be laid down, and then the "hands" of tobacco piled upon it crosswise in successive layers, and lapping each other about three or four inches at the points of the leaves. If "bulked" beside a wall, a space must be left behind for air to pass through to prevent moulding. It may be thus "bulked" four or five feet in height without danger of spoiling. In most sections the crop is sold to merchants who have packing houses, and who pack it in cases of about three hundred pounds each, and store it until it has gone through the "sweating" process, by which it becomes fit for manufacturing purposes, and then dispose of it to manufacturers and speculators in the city markets.

PACKING.

In order to transport it more readily, it is put up in bales of about one hundred pounds each. The process of baling is performed thus: make a bottomless box about thirty-four inches long (inside) by sixteen high and wide. On each side nail two upright cleats, one-and-a-half inches thick, each ten inches from the end. Across these cleats, parallel and even with the top of the box, nail a narrow strip of board. These strips or rails are to confine and keep the ends of the straw-bands out of the way while packing. Now have a duplicate box the same size in length and breadth, but about six inches deep, to fit down on the top of the first box; there must be three notches cut in the bottom of each side of this box for the bands to pass through. It should fit down close on the top of the true box. There must also be a lid made to slip up and down easily in the box, with three notches in each side to allow it to slip past the bands. When ready to pack, have good bands made of rye-straw, and wet, to render them more pliable. Twist them, and getting inside the box, lay one band down on the ground, with the knot in the middle, and within three inches of the end of the box, and place one foot in each corner of the box upon the band, then push the ends of the band down between the outside of the box and the rail. There must be three bands in all, one at each end and one in the middle. When the bands are in the box, the " hands " of tobacco are laid in the same as in the " bulk," keeping the ends of the bunches well against the end of the box until it is filled, then put on the lid and press it down with lever or screw, whichever may be most convenient; after it is pressed sufficiently solid remove the lid and place the upper box in its proper position, fill up to the top with tobacco, and press it down again, and so until the box is sufficiently full to come within the limits of the bands to confine. Now remove the upper box and tie the middle band first (this prevents the mass from expanding further), and lastly the end ones, and give it another pressure to set the bands and restore the shape of the bale; now pull off the box and there remains a neat, square bale of tobacco of about one hundred pounds' weight, that will bear handling and transportation almost anywhere without injury or coming open. If the tobacco should become too dry in the " bulk " to pack, it may be restored by sprinkling it lightly with hot water, using a small corn-broom, and "rebulking" it, taking down and sprinkling one layer at a time, and allowing it to remain about two days, when the water will have become diffused throughout the whole, and it again be fit to pack.

RICHMOND INTERESTS.

In an interest in which North Carolina is so largely connected with the Virginia markets, it would be unjust to pass by the relation in which Richmond stands to those interests. For two hundred years she has been the arbiter of the tobacco markets, controlling them by the influence of character and experience. Those interests are extended over so much ground that it is not proposed, from the magnitude of the subject, to more than refer to the subject. As identified with North Carolina interests an exception is made in the case of Messrs. Hill, Skinker & Watkins, two of whom are North Carolinians, one a Virginian, but all animated by the finest North Carolina spirit.

Their business was established in 1866. Charles D. Hill and Charles Watkins, native North Carolinians, from Caswell County in this State, have literally spent their lives from early boyhood handling the bright tobacco which originated in their county. The senior partner, Mr. C. D. Hill, went to Richmond early after the completion of the R. & D. R. R. in 1857, and has been identified with the tobacco trade of that city ever since, except the period covered by the late civil war.

This house has been thoroughly identified with the bright tobacco interest of North Carolina in all the stages of its development, and are now handling it probably to as large an extent as any one house in the United States, and have done as much as any one house to introduce North Carolina's great staple to the notice of tobacco dealers and manufacturers as any one house in the trade.

Their buildings, erected for warehouse purposes on Carey street, are no doubt the best in Virginia, erected with special reference to the preservation of the peculiar qualities of the special tobacco they control ; especially of brights, which change color less and keep longer than the same tobacco stored in ordinary sheds. The centre warehouse is of brick two and a half stories high, 80 feet front, running back 260 feet, and are in all respects perfectly adapted to the uses to which they are appropriated.

Parrish & Blackwell,

DURHAM, N. C.,

Wholesale Leaf Tobacco Dealers.

LARGEST DEALERS IN NORTH CAROLINA !

Deal Exclusively in the Celebrated Tobacco grown in the "Golden Belt of North Carolina."

FINE AND FANCY BRIGHT WRAPPERS AND SMOKERS

A SPECIALTY !

All our Goods Warranted to come Fully up to Sample !

All Short and Inferior Tobacco thrown out. Every Package prized thoroughly uniform and our name stencilled thereon.

You will find our goods on sale at Louisville, St. Louis, New York and Richmond.

ALWAYS GIVES SATISFACTION.

GRAVES' WAREHOUSE,

DANVILLE, VA.

STILL OFFERS

Superior Advantages for Storing, Handling and the SALE of

LEAF TOBACCO.

We have Good Lights and Good Accommodations, with a polite and experienced corps of gentlemen, who will at all times give strict attention to handling and the sale of all Tobacco sent to this house.

We will furnish Tierces at any Railroad Station upon application, and will use our best efforts to obtain the

HIGHEST MARKET PRICES

for your Tobacco.

WM. P. GRAVES, - - Proprietor.

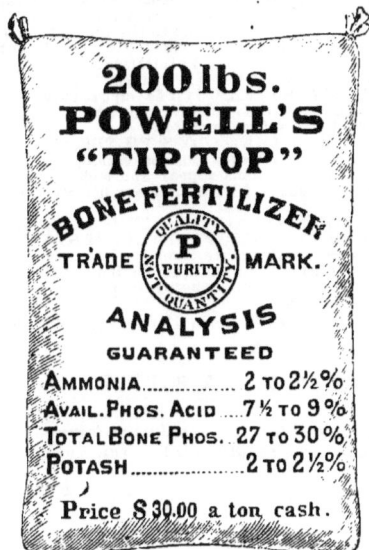

OF SPECIAL INTEREST

TO THE

Tobacco Growers of North Carolina!

The bulk of the Tobacco now produced in North Carolina is of the yellow types, and the success attending its cultivation has been such as to induce us to look for a still further extension of its range. The Southern Fertilizing Company, of Richmond, Va., early appreciating the probable progress of this industry, not only prepared a fertilizer that would produce yellow leaf of the finest quality, but supplied the grower needing information with the fullest instructions how to handle the crop from the seed-bed to the warehouse. It is every way desirable that North Carolina should *maintain* her reputation as the home of the finest yellow tobacco in the world. The fertilizer her people use on this crop should be one that time has *proven* to be *entirely reliable.* This proof is shown by the

"Anchor  **Brand."**

It has been fourteen years in the field, and continues to stand *without a rival* on fine yellow tobacco. Hear what is said about it by MAJOR ROBERT L. RAGLAND, of Halifax County, Va., who is accepted on all hands as the best tobacco authority in the United States:

" There are several brands of fertilizers manufactured specially for tobacco, differing in composition, price and merit ; and after repeated experiments with most if not all of the best, the author gives it as his decided opinion, that for *fine, bright, silky tobacco* nothing equals the Anchor Brand Tobacco Fertilizer, prepared by the Southern Fertilizing Company, Richmond, Va. And this opinion is based upon fourteen years' trial, and often in competition with the best of other brands on the market. It is a *tried and proved* fertilizer, which the planter can use without the risk of getting something unsuited to his crop; and therefore I can recommend it with confidence."

This Standard Fertilizer is for Sale at every important point in North Carolina.

ENQUIRE AND YOU WILL FIND IT.

ASHEVILLE WAREHOUSE

FOR THE SALE OF

LEAF TOBACCO

WILLOW STREET,

Opposite Eagle Hotel,   **ASHEVILLE, N. C.**

HIGHEST MARKET PRICES, AND BEST ATTENTION TO
MAN AND TEAMS GUARANTEED.

ALSO AGENT FOR

ALLISON & ADDISON

"STAR BRAND" FERTILIZER

THE COMPLETE TOBACCO MANURE.

Containing, by Analysis, the following Elements Absolutely Essential for the
Production of

PERFECT TOBACCO!

AMMONIA,	2 to 4 per cent.
PHOSPHORIC ACID, Soluble,	4 to 8 "
PHOSPHORIC ACID, Insoluble,	6 to 8 "
SULPHATE POTASH,	3 to 5 "

BYNUM, COTTEN & JONES,

WINSTON, N. C.

MANUFACTURERS OF FINE CHEWING TOBACCOS

LEADING BRANDS:

NO NAME, SILVER WAVE, SMART ELICK, OUR NED, WACHOVIA, MAMIE LEE.

CORRESPONDENCE SOLICITED.—Buyers quoted same prices as if personally present.

PIEDMONT WAREHOUSE

WINSTON, N. C.

Stands in the front rank with none ahead. Sales for the present year more than thirty thousand (30,000) parcels. Increase in past four years more than four fold. Hundreds of new customers have been added during present year; still there is room for more. With many thanks for past patronage, we ask a liberal share in the future.

M. W. NORFLEET,

PROPRIETOR OF

PIEDMONT WAREHOUSE

THE FOLLOWING NAMED GENTLEMEN ARE STILL WITH ME:

W. A. S. PEARCE,	JAMES S. SCALES,	J. Q. A. BARHAM,
BOOK-KEEPER.	FLOOR MANAGER.	AUCTIONEER.

OCTOBER 1st, 1880.

I. E. RAY,

ASHEVILLE, - - NORTH CAROLINA.

"Without a Rival !"

IS SAID OF

WESTERN NORTH CAROLINA TOBACCO

IN THE VIRGINIA MARKETS.

It has taken a PREMIUM in the GREAT TOBACCO MART of the UNITED STATES !

AND AGAIN AT THE

Great Páris Exposition over the Tobaccos of the World !

THE BEST KNOWN BRANDS OF SMOKING TOBACCO !

"Asheville's Best"

AND

"Black Mountain,"

Manufactured by I. E. RAY,

Of PURE NORTH CAROLINA LEAF, and peculiarly adapted to the Pipe; are already famous and sought as the most desirable, in fact, it is said that nowhere else can such be had.

Among all the good things that give life its zest,
These famous Tobaccos now rival the best.

SEND FOR SAMPLE.

JOHN A. LEE.   *Established 1841.*   J. OTEY TAYLOR.

LEE, TAYLOR & CO.,

LEAF TOBACCO

AND

PRODUCE COMMISSION MERCHANTS,

Office, No. 66 Main St.,

LYNCHBURG, VA.

The publishers of this pamphlet copy from the "Lynchburg Virginian," of October 27, 1880, the following notice in reference to the above firm:

LYNCHBURG ENTERPRISE.—*Notes of a Prosperous House and its Business.*—One of the best known and most deservedly popular business houses in Virginia is that now known as Lee, Taylor & Co.. Leaf Tobacco and Produce Commission Merchants, 66 Main street. The history of this establishment makes an interesting and important part of that of Lynchburg itself. It has grown, like the city, if not slowly at least surely, and the various changes through which the business has passed are well worth recording:

In 1841 the firm of Roberts & Lee was established when the city and its trade may be said to have been in their infancy, compared with the present proportions, and their business, though small, was lucrative, and the partnership continued until 1844, when the firm of Lee & Roberts was formed and continued until 1847; then they were succeeded by McDaniel & Lee. This firm continued in active business until 1853, when Lee & Johnson stepped forward and conducted the business until 1859. Then came Lee, Rocke & Taylor, whose partnership was not dissolved until 1865. Then Lee & Taylor conducted the business until 1870, when the firm name was changed to Lee, Taylor & Co., and this partnership continued for three years. In 1873 the firm was again changed to Lee & Taylor Bros., and, in 1879, to Lee, Taylor & Payne. And now, October, 1880, the firm is again known as Lee, Taylor & Co., as it was ten years ago, Mr. Mosby H. Payne having retired.

It may be mentioned, as a significant proof of the energy, tact and popularity of the numerous business men who have from time to time been members of this firm, which dates back nearly forty years, that though the business was originally small, every successive firm has increased its trade and popularity, and that, in all these long years, and amid all the changes and vicissitudes which have wrecked many business establishments, this house has never failed to pay any note or other obligation at maturity, and has never asked indulgence from a creditor, while granting that favor with a liberal hand to its customers and debtors.

An idea of the immense business of this house may be gathered from the fact that during the past year they sold at their warehouse (Martin's) over six and a half millions pounds of tobacco, being more than one-fourth of all sold in the market. Their dealings with producers, buyers and consumers have been so satisfactory as to increase their trade and make new friends and patrons every month.

From the small beginning of forty years ago, this house has established not only an enormous retail trade, but wholesale patronage which is surprising—their business last year aggregating a half million dollars; and to demonstrate "how pleasant it is for brethren to dwell together in unity," it may be stated that the present proprietors have been together more than twenty years.

In view of a large expected increase of business in future they have greatly increased their facilities for accommodating the wants of all their patrons. The farmer who wants seed grain need go no further to find everything in that line that the market affords, for in this specialty Lee, Taylor & Co. have no opposition. In field seeds, some other firms here make the competition lively.

In addition to their enormous leaf tobacco, commission and grocery business, this firm are also sole agents for Dupont & Co.'s powder and fuse of all grades. In fact anything to be found in a wholesale grocery and commission house will be promptly supplied by them on terms as reasonable as any other house can offer.

We have thus hastily and imperfectly alluded to the claims of this house upon the patronage and confidence of the public, with no other desire than to call attention to a deserving enterprise which fully demonstrates its claims to continued support.

123

J. C. & D. Y. COOPER,
PROPRIETORS OF
COOPER'S WAREHOUSE,
HENDERSON. N. C.

The Largest & Best Arranged Warehouse in North Carolina for Showing Fine Tobacco.

All grades of Tobacco sold for Full Market Value. Strict personal attention given to Weighing and Selling. Prompt payments and returns made after each sale, either in Currency or Checks, as planters may desire. Ample Camp Lots and Sheds for the protection of Stock. Our demand for Fine Wrappers, Smokers and Fillers is large and increasing, at Full Prices.
No. 1 Peruvian Guano, Ober's Tobacco Compound, and Buggies, Carriages and Wagons always on hand at Rock Bottom Prices.

J. S. LOCKHART,
DEALER IN
LEAF TOBACCO
DURHAM, N. C.

ORDERS SOLICITED, SATISFACTION GUARANTEED.
SMOKERS A SPECIALTY.

REFER BY PERMISSION:—W. T. Blackwell & Co., Durham, N. C. A. Y. Stokes & Co., Richmond, Va. Pace, Bro. & Co., Lynchburg, Va. Spaulding & Merrick, Chicago. J. E. Venable & Son, Petersburg, Va.

DR. G. W. BLACKNALL—NEW MOREHEAD CITY HOTEL.—The public will be delighted to know that the new Hotel at Morehead City has been leased by Dr. G. W. Blacknall, proprietor of the Yarboro House, Raleigh, N. C., for the period of five years. Dr. Blacknall is widely known as the best hotel man in North Carolina. No man in the hotel annals of the State has ever been known to handle a crowd with so much ease as he. By the coming season there will be good accommodations for five or six hundred guests. This most excellent House is fitted up with every modern improvement. The ball-room will be the largest and best arranged in the United States. Every room will be supplied with gas and water. This hotel is beautifully and conveniently situated near the water edge, and is one of the most agreeable places for the seaside visitor on the Atlantic coast. We bespeak for the Doctor a most successful season for the coming summer.—*The Torchlight*, Oxford, N. C.

HORNER SCHOOL,

OXFORD, N. C.

A Classical, Mathematical, Scientific, and English School, with Military Organization and Discipline.

PRINCIPALS:

JAMES H. HORNER, A. M. | JEROME C. HORNER, A. M.

ASSISTANT INSTRUCTORS:

J. P. PAISLEY, A. B.,
Latin, Greek, Mathematics, and English Branches.

TH. V. JASMUND, Ph. D.,
French, German, Geography and History.

No expense or pains will be spared to maintain the high reputation of the

HORNER SCHOOL,

and to make it complete in all the requirements of a first-rate preparatory and finishing Academy.

The elder MR. HORNER has had a varied experience of thirty years in the schoolroom; and his son, MR. J. C. HORNER, after the best preparatory training under his father, was graduated with distinction at Davidson College, since which time he has been constantly engaged in teaching.

None but well-qualified Assistant Instructors will be employed; and none but honorable and studious boys will be ret ined in the school.

The location is retired, but not so remote from the town as to lose the healthful influence of its refined society. Students live in the family of the Principals; and their conduct out of school and in school is strictly supervised and controlled. The standard of scholarship and of gentlemanly deportment is high.

The course of study is complete. The Text-Books are up to the latest advancements in every department; and the best educational advantages in all the appointments of the School are provided. The session is divided into two terms of twenty weeks each, with only one day's interval.

The first term of the scholastic year begins the third Monday in August; the second, the first Tuesday in January.

The charge for board and tuition is $100 for each session, or $200 for the whole scholastic year, payable at the beginning of each term.

For further particulars apply to

JEROME C. HORNER,
OXFORD, N. C.

THE OXONIAN,

A Journal of Literature and Education,

Published Monthly, at Oxford, N. C., at One Dollar a Year, in advance.

Offers decided advantages to advertisers. High average circulation. Advertisements shown prominently, are free from errors and are tastefully displayed. Its advertising rates are not in excess of its value to an advertiser. Advertisements, intended for publication in any issue, should be in the office by the 20th of the month.

J. C. HORNER, OXFORD, N. C.

THE
HUNDLEY TOBACCO ORDERER.

This is undoubtedly one of the greatest conveniences for the Tobacco Farmer yet invented. By its use the farmer is enabled to remove his tobacco immediately after it is cured in any kind of weather without the least damage.

He can strip and market his crop at any time or during any season, and especially is it useful in cold rainy weather, when it is too disagreeable to work out of doors, and too cold for tobacco to soften.

Every man that has handled leaf tobacco knows the many advantages derived from a method by which it can be softened, at any time, without damage, and only needs to be assured that the

HUNDLEY TOBACCO ORDERER

will do this, and he will at once appreciate its value.

With our *Improved Orderer* we have never failed to give satisfaction, and can produce more than one hundred testimonials, but for want of space confine ourselves to a few from the leading farmers in different localities.

TESTIMONIALS.

Letter from F. J. Tilley, of Knap of Reeds, N. C., to W. A. Davis, Editor of the Oxford " Torch-Light ":

* * * * * * As fine yellow tobacco is so much more profitable than any other kind, it is not only best to know how to cure it bright, but also how to retain the fancy color. Every person at all acquainted with the nature of fine yellow tobacco knows that it is liable and apt to change if allowed to soften too much or too quickly; therefore, it is important not to allow it to undergo any change that will cause it to lose its fancy color. Having some experience with fine tobacco myself, I went to see what effect the Orderer had upon tobacco, and whether or not it would change the color. We put some very fine into the barn, which was entirely dry. I examined it well, and when it was thoroughly softened, I found that the color was not changed in the least. I continued to experiment until I was perfectly convinced that it would not at all change the most fancy color. It required about thirty-five minutes to soften the leaf, but would take some time longer to soften the large stems sufficiently to strip. I am perfectly satisfied that the Orderer will not change the color any more than a natural season. It is arranged to distribute the steam uniformly over the barn, and can be easily turned on or off. Tobacco can be softened or ordered by it quickly or slowly, as may suit best.

Knap of Reeds, July 17th, 1880.   F. J. TILLY.

WINSTEAD, PERSON COUNTY, N. C.,
June 10th, 1880.

DEAR SIR:

Herewith find orders for five of your Tobacco Orderers. * * The tobacco you ordered when here I sent to Danville a few days after you left. *The warehousemen pronounced the order good.* From what I have seen of the Orderer I am more than satisfied that it is an indispensable adjunct to every tobacco farm, and that in the course of a few years every man that raises fine tobacco will have one. I am now satisfied, from my experience, that it will not change the color or in any other way damage fine tobacco. Wishing you much success, I remain

Yours truly,   A. J. HESTER.

WINSTEAD, PERSON COUNTY, N. C.

J. C. HUNDLEY, Esq., Oxford, N. C.   October 18th, 1880.

Dear Sir:—Your Improved Tobacco Orderers have given general satisfaction so far. Many farmers signify their intention of purchasing at an early date. * * They all work charmingly. * * Make two more for me. Very truly,

A. J. HESTER.

RIDGEWAY, WARREN Co , N. C., Sept. 9, 1880.

MR. J. C. HUNDLEY.

Dear Sir:—I received the Orderer you sent. It worked very well. I have sold it and wish you to send me another. I would like to take the agency for this county. Very respectfully,   T. B. WATSON.

CEDAR GROVE, ORANGE Co., N. C., Sept. 15th, 1880.

MR. J. C. HUNDLEY,

Dear Sir:—I am glad to hear that you are receiving so many orders for your Orderer, feeling certain that it is just what every tobacco farmer needs. I am using mine and it works well.   Respectfully yours,   W. H. ANDERSON.

OXFORD, N. C., July 8th, 1880.

MR. J. C. HUNDLEY.

Dear Sir:—I have been using the Steam Orderer I bought of you, and am well pleased with it. I think I can recommend it to do what you claim for it. It will order tobacco in a very little time and uniformly through the house. Very respectfully,   FIELDING KNOTT.

OXFORD, N. C., Nov. 23d, 1880.

I have thoroughly examined the Hundley Tobacco Orderer and know it to be a complete success. No tobacco farmer can afford to be without one. He can often save the cost of one in a single load of tobacco by being able to handle it at any time.

H. G. COOPER, Proprietor of Cooper's Warehouse.

OUR RIGHTS are protected by Letters Patent, number 224,290, bearing date February 10th, 1880, and covering the process of ordering Leaf Tobacco by passing the steam from a suitable boiler through a pipe perforated in such a manner that the main portion of the steam issues in a direction away from the overhanging tobacco.

Any infringements on our rights will be speedily and vigorously prosecuted.

Good responsible Agents wanted in every tobacco section in the United States.

We will sell State, County, Township or Farm Rights.

For terms and other information address,

"The Hundley Tobacco Orderer Company,"

OXFORD, GRANVILLE CO., N. C.

"DURHAM RECORDER,"

DURHAM, N. C.

OLDEST PAPER IN NORTH CAROLINA!

Published at Tobacco Headquarters by

J. D. CAMERON, - - - *Editor & Propriet r.*

PRICE, $1.50 PER YEAR.

TOBACCO SEED GIVEN AWAY!

TO EVERY NEW SUBSCRIBER TO

THE TORCH LIGHT,

OXFORD, N. C.

We will present a package of Major Ragland's Tobacco Seed, of either of the popular varieties:

YELLOW ORONOKO, YELLOW PRYOR,
BIG ORONOKO, GOLD LEAF,
SWEET ORONOKO, WHITE BURLEY.

The Torch Light is Published every Tuesday Morning, at Oxford, N. C., by W. A. Davis, at the price of

$1.50 PER YEAR.

Oxford is in the Centre of the finest tobacco region in the world.

A large Weekly Family, News and Literary Paper. The best advertising medium in North Carolina.

Address **W. A. DAVIS, Editor and Prop.,**

OXFORD, N. C.

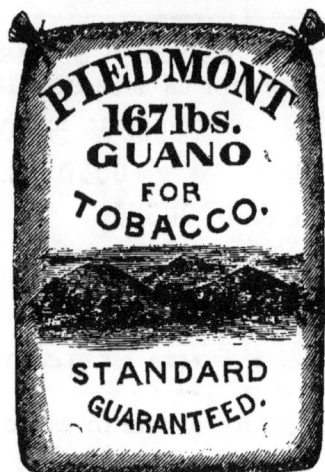

W. T. BLACKWELL & CO.,

DURHAM, NORTH CAROLINA,

MANUFACTURERS OF THE ONLY

Genuine Durham Smoking Tobacco.

BLACKWELL'S DURHAM

Is the FINEST, PUREST, BEST, and most uniform Brand of Smoking Tobacco ever put upon the Market.

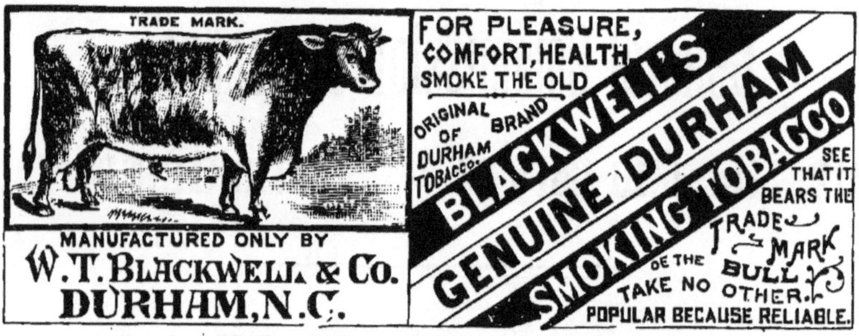

ALSO MANUFACTURERS OF

Durham Long Cut and Durham Cigarettes.

THESE GOODS WE OFFER UNDER AN ABSOLUTE GUARANTEE

THAT

They are the Finest and Purest Gooas upon the Market.
They are free from Drugs or Chemicals of any kind.
They consist of the Finest Tobacco, and Purest Rice Paper made.

SEND US YOUR ORDERS.

SATISFACTION GUARANTEED.

* 9 7 8 3 3 3 7 3 0 6 5 9 5 *